# IDYLLS OF FARRINGFORD

A Biographical study of

ALFRED, LORD TENNYSON
in the Isle of Wight
with Selected Poems.

Born at Somersby, Lincolnshire - August 6th, 1809
Moved into Farringford, Isle of Wight - 1853
Died at Aldworth, near Haslemere - October 6th, 1892

Richard J. Hutchings

# OTHER HUNNYHILL PUBLICATIONS

*Richard J. Hutchings*
Dickens on an Island
The Wordsworth Poetical Guide to the Lakes
Pot Pourri of Poems RJH

*Richard J. Hutchings and Dr. Raymond V. Turley*
Young Algernon Swinburne

*Elizabeth Hutchings*
Discovering the Sculptures of George Frederick Watts
Gardening for Lily - The story of an organic garden and its family
Busts & Titbits - Woolner Busts & Freshwater Fragments

*Hester Thackeray Fuller*
Three Freshwater Friends - Tennyson, Watts and Mrs. Cameron

*Joan Brading Grayer*
I Lived in Julia's House

*By the author with Dr. Brian Hinton M.B.E.*
The Journal of Emily Tennyson 1853 - 1864
Published by The Isle of Wight County Press

First Edition 1965
2nd Edition 1998
Reprinted 2002
Reprinted 2006

©Richard J. Hutchings

ISBN 0 9521939 4 9

Published by Hunnyhill Publications,
2 Gate House, Gate Lane, Freshwater Bay, Isle of Wight, PO40 9QT
Tel: (01983) 759090   Email: e.hutchings@talktalk.net

Printed by Biltmore Printers
14 Manners View, Newport, Isle of Wight, PO30 5FA

# CONTENTS

. . . . .

| | |
|---|---|
| THE ROMANTIC LEGACY — INTRODUCTORY . . . . | 4 |
| I HAVE LED HER HOME, MY LOVE . . . . . | 19 |
| GOD-GIFTED ORGAN-VOICE OF ENGLAND . . . . | 29 |
| MY OWN IDEAL KNIGHT . . . . . . . | 35 |
| THE SEA FROM MAIDEN'S CROFT . . . . . | 41 |
| SUNSET AND EVENING STAR . . . . . . | 45 |
| KING ALFRED . . . . . . . . . | 49 |
| MEMOIRS OF FRIENDS AND NEIGHBOURS OF FARRINGFORD | 55 |
| BEYOND THE GRAVE (From Hallam Tennyson's *Memoir*). | 62 |

. . . . .

## POEMS BY TENNYSON

POEMS DESCRIPTIVE OF FARRINGFORD:
| | |
|---|---|
| *To The Rev. F. D. Maurice* . . . . . . | 15 |
| *To Gifford Palgrave* . . . . . . . | 17 |

POEMS QUOTED IN TEXT:
| | |
|---|---|
| *The Poet* (extract) . . . . . . . . | 6 |
| *Ulysses* (extract) . . . . . . . . | 10 |
| *Prologue* (from "In Memoriam") . . . . . | 11 |
| *Maud* (various extracts) . . . . . . | 20 - 27 |
| *In The Garden of Swainston* . . . . . . | 28 |
| *The Charge of the Light Brigade* . . . . . | 31 |
| *Guinevere* (extract) . . . . . . . | 33 |
| *Dedication* (from the "Idylls of the King") . . | 39 |
| *Enoch Arden* (various extracts) . . . . . | 42 - 44 |
| *Crossing the Bar* . . . . . . . . | 46 |
| *Tears, Idle Tears* . . . . . . . . | 54 |

SELECTED POEMS PUBLISHED AFTER 1853:
| | |
|---|---|
| *Come Into The Garden, Maud* (from "Maud") . . | 64 |
| *The Holy Grail* (extract) . . . . . . | 67 |
| *The Passing of Arthur* (extract) . . . . . | 71 |
| *To the Marquis of Dufferin and Ava* . . . . | 78 |

# THE ROMANTIC LEGACY — INTRODUCTORY

W<small>HEN</small> Tennyson was born in 1809, the great *Lyrical Ballads,* of Wordsworth and Coleridge, was only twelve years old. But by then the republican ideals generated in the Romantic poets by the French Revolution of 1789, had soured with disillusionment.

French hopes for "Liberty, Equality, and Fraternity," which had echoed excitingly in the hearts of all just Englishmen, were, by the beginning of the nineteenth century, seen to be nothing more than the springs of a new tyranny far bloodier than anything Europe had ever known. Cheated now of the fulfilment of their democratic dreams, Englishmen no longer cared for the fate of their society.

As early as 1802 Wordsworth was crying in anguish to the spirit of a Milton to save England. from her torpor, from the spiritual, intellectual and moral degeneracy that was everywhere evident—

> Milton! thou shouldst be living at this hour:
> England hath need of thee: she is a fen
> Of stagnant waters: altar, sword, and pen,
> Fireside, the heroic wealth of hall and bower,
> Have forfeited their ancient English dower
> Of inward happiness. We are selfish men . . . .

And a few years later a younger generation in Byron and Shelley also began waging private wars against the social systems of their day.

Keats, with his plaintive "Glory and loveliness have passed away," preferred to bury his head in the golden sands of ancient Greek mythology. Who can blame him, for he was not physically or intellectually equipped to be a prophet and leader of England in her troubled times?

By 1824 all three of the youngest Romantics had died tragically in voluntary exile. Coleridge lingered on, his best poetry written and his Muse seeking solace now in opium, until 1834. Alone, of the five Romantic poets, Wordsworth lived out his fourscore years until 1850, gradually settling into the conservatism of old age.

But though lacking in fire and militant idealism, he found new spiritual comfort and greatness in a wider philosophical view of Man and the Universe from the seclusion of his Lakeland mountains.

He was respected above all other living English poets. So much so that when Robert Southey, the Poet Laureate, died in 1843, Queen Victoria did not hesitate to offer him the post. Grudgingly he accepted the appointment, but never honoured it by composing a single laureate ode, and, indeed, only attended one levee at the Palace.

The first thirty years of the century had been "narrow times, narrow spiritually, narrow politically." Let us alone, Englishmen said, bother us no more with your high ideals that do not work out in practice. Look where such ill-conceived dreams have led Europe now. We will not be taken in a second time.

In those years too, the voice of the poets was unheard. Neither could the Anglican Church offer any inspiring leadership. England, like the Ancient Mariner, might have cried,

> And Christ would take no pity on
>   My soul in agony . . .
> I look'd to Heaven, and try'd to pray;
>   But or ever a prayer had gusht,
> A wicked whisper came and made
>   My heart as dry as dust.

Tennyson understood well that England's greatest spiritual need was the reaffirmation of basic Christian beliefs, and only in this way could she rid herself of the cursed Albatross of her troubled conscience. The Poet with his deep religious faith, sensed that it was in him to do this, but his first volume of poetry, *Poems by Two Brothers* (written in 1826 in collaboration with two of his brothers), influenced strongly by Byron's work, showed he was not yet ready for the task.

**Religious, Social and Poetical Awakening**
The long-awaited Social Reform came in the 'thirties, followed soon by the High Church and Broad Church movements of the Anglican faith. And it was really during this exciting new era of spiritual rebirth that the poetical careers of Tennyson and Browning began. Tennyson expresses wonderfully in *The Poet,* the resurgence of new political ideals:

> And Freedom rear'd in that august sunrise
>   Her beautiful bold brow,
> When rites and forms before his burning eyes
>   Melted like snow.
>
> There was no blood upon her maiden robes
>   Sunn'd by those orient skies;
> But round about the circles of the globes
>   Of her keen eyes
>
> And in her raiment's hem was traced in flame
>   *WISDOM,* a name to shake
> All evil dreams of power—a sacred name.
>   And when she spake,
>
> Her words did gather thunder as they ran,
>   And as the lightning to the thunder
> Which follows it, riving the spirit of man,
>   Making earth wonder,
>
> So was their meaning to her words. No sword
>   Of wrath her right arm whirl'd,
> But one poor poet's scroll, and with *his* word
>   She shook the world.

"This religious awakening," said Stopford Brooke, "was felt and seized by two distinct types of character, or of human tendency, and crystallised by two representative men, by J. H. Newman and Frederick Maurice [both friends of Tennyson]; and it is curious for those who care for analogies to the evolution of species to trace how the one was the child of the University of Oxford and the other of the University of Cambridge. The main difference which lay between their method of presenting the faith was a time-difference, if I may be allowed to invent that term. In the matter of religion the past was the foremost thing to Newman, to Maurice the present. Newman looked back to the past (the nearer to the Apostles the nearer to truth) for the highest point to which religious life, but not doctrine, had attained, and his immense reverence for the past became part of the mind of Tennyson. But it was balanced in Tennyson by even a greater reverence for the present as containing in it an immediate inspiration and revelation from God. This foundation for poetic thought and emotion was given to him by the religious work of Maurice. The deepest thought in the mind of Maurice was that God was moving in the present as fully as He had moved in the past; and the incessant representation of this, in every form of it, was his great contribution to Theology."

The necessary vitality of the present, the deep need for high poetic work—man alive and Nature alive with the life of God—which were Maurice's doctrine, were to influence Tennyson's poetry until his death in 1892.

## The Influence of Keats

Tennyson's roots were in the Romantic Revival, and it is not surprising that he was, in his youth, captivated by Byron's virile style and romantic individualism, as he was by Shelley's splendour and colour. But he was soon to reject their influence.

Of the five Romantic poets, he found most to admire and emulate in the oldest and the youngest of their number—Wordsworth for his breadth of vision but essential simplicity, and Keats for his sublime dedication to beauty and Nature. In his wisdom he chose Keats's work, primarily, as a corner stone upon which to erect the edifice of his own poetic genius.

"Keats," he once remarked, "would have become one of the very greatest of all poets, had he lived. At the time of his death there was apparently no sign of exhaustion or having written himself out; his keen poetical instinct was in full process of development at the time. Each new effort was a steady advance on that which had gone before."

Sir Alfred Lyall points out that "it was Keats who, as Tennyson's forerunner, passed on to him the gift of intense romantic susceptibilities to the influences of Nature, the 'dim mystic sympathies with tree and hill reaching back into childhood.' But Tennyson's art inclined more towards the picturesque, towards using words, as a painter uses his brush, for producing the impression of a scene's true outline and colour; his work shows the realistic feeling of a later day, which delights in precision of details."

This realism and precision of detail were signs of the times. New scientific knowledge and discoveries, and the rapid expansion and development of Britain's colonies, were awakening influences which were reflected in the poet's work.

Tennyson, Lyall said, managed to illustrate symbolically some mental state or emotion, availing himself of the mysterious relation between man and his environment, whereby the outer inanimate world is felt to be the resemblance and reflection of human moods.

**Coleridge's Criticism of his Work**
As Coleridge died in 1834, he could only have seen Tennyson's immature work, which he once criticised. Tennyson remembering this in later years, in conversation with Coleridge's nephew, Arthur, said he knew why his uncle had done so: "Your uncle's words: 'Tennyson has no sense of rhythm and scansion,' have been constantly quoted against me. The truth is that in my youth I used no hyphens in writing composite words, and the reader might fancy that from this omission I had no knowledge of the length and measure of words and expressions."

But there were others, like Thackeray, A. H. Hallam, James Spedding, Edward FitzGerald and Lushington, his contemporaries at Cambridge University, who, even in those early days, saw in him great promise as a poet and thinker.

**Tennyson's Characteristics**
The Poet had several characteristics that were the hall-marks of greatness. The Rev. H. Montagu Butler summed them up in

later years, by saying that he was "simple, natural, shrewd, humorous; feeling strongly on a vast variety of subjects, and saying freely what he felt; passing rapidly and easily from the gravest matters of speculation or conduct to some trifling or amusing incident of the moment, or some recollection of the years of his youth; he seemed to me unconscious of being a great man, though he must have known himself to be one of the foremost thinkers, and quite the foremost poet of his day. He was wholly free from affectation. He was never an actor of a part. There was about him always an atmosphere of truth.

'Truth-teller was our Alfred named,'

was a line that again and again recurred to the memory as one heard him speak out his mind either on men, or on politics, or on the deepest mysteries of philosophy or religion. He was preeminently one of the Children of Light. Of light, whether from science, or from literary criticism, or from the progress of the human conscience, he hailed thankfully and expectantly every fresh disclosure. There was a deep reverence in him for the Unseen, the Undiscovered, the as yet Unrevealed. This on the intellectual side; and on the moral side there was a manly, a devout, and a tender veneration for purity and innocence and truthfulness, and, to borrow his own stately words, written early in his life:

'Self-reverence, self knowledge, self-control.' "

## The Death of Hallam

The death of his dearest friend Arthur Henry Hallam, in 1833, was to shake the foundations of his religious faith violently, and was to scar his memory with sadness at the loss of a man who would have risen to greatness.

Soon afterwards Tennyson began work on a poem (*In Memoriam*), dedicated to Hallam, which in every word showed how desperate had been the struggle to preserve his faith, to free himself from the slough of despond, and to view his life more philosophically. Year by year he worked on the poem, and all the while his art and his intellect matured as he progressed with it. By 1842 he had found self-reverence, self-knowledge, self-control, and he could look outward, with greater confidence, to the world around him—

> Come, my friends,
> 'Tis not too late to seek a newer world.
> Push off, and sitting well in order smite
> The sounding furrows; for my purpose holds
> To sail beyond the sunset, and the baths
> Of all the western stars, until I die.
> It may be that the gulfs will wash us down:
> It may be we shall touch the Happy Isles,
> And see the great Achilles, whom we knew.
> Tho' much is taken, much abides; and tho'
> We are not now that strength which in old days
> Moved earth and heaven; that which we are, we are;
> One equal temper of heroic hearts,
> Made weak by time and fate, but strong in will
> To strive, to seek, to find, and not to yield.     (*Ulysses*)

## Year of Destiny
Meanwhile Wordsworth still lived and remained the remote literary figure-head of the day. Tennyson was relatively unknown as yet, poor as a church-mouse, and, because of that, prevented for twelve years from marrying his betrothed, Emily Sellwood. Then suddenly in 1850, the tide in Tennyson's affairs turned, and taken at the flood, led on to fortune.

## In Memoriam
By 1849 he had put the finishing touches to the "Prologue" of *In Memoriam*, and the completed work was published in the following year. Swiftly, within a period of twelve months, his financial position improved, he married Emily, Wordsworth died and he was appointed Poet Laureate in his place. The Queen's decision to make him laureate on the merits of this poem, reflected great credit on her understanding of the mood of her people at the time, and her realisation that they were desperately in need of spiritual, moral and literary leadership.

As Sir Alfred Lyall put it: "The profound impression that was immediately produced by these exquisitely musical meditations may be ascribed, we think, to their sympathetic association with the spiritual needs and intellectual dilemmas of the time . . . . It strengthened the impulse to go onward trustfully; but it may also be counted among the indirect influences which combined to promote the notable reaction toward the sacramental and mysterious side of religion, toward positive faith as the safeguard of morals, which has been the outcome of the great Anglican revival set. on foot by the Oxford Movement . . . ."

## From **IN MEMORIAM**
### The Prologue

Strong Son of God, immortal Love,
    Whom we, that have not seen thy face,
    By faith, and faith alone, embrace,
Believing where we cannot prove;

Thine are these orbs of light and shade;
    Thou madest Life in man and brute;
    Thou madest Death; and 10, thy foot
Is on the skull which thou hast made.

Thou wilt not leave us in the dust:
    Thou madest man, he knows not why;
    He thinks he was not made to die;
And thou hast made him: thou art just.

Thou seemest human and divine,
    The highest, holiest manhood, thou:
    Our wills are ours, we know not how;
Our wills are ours, to make them thine.

Our little systems have their day;
    They have their day and cease to be:
    They are but broken lights of thee,
And thou, O Lord, art more than they.

We have but faith: we cannot know;
    For knowledge is of things we see;
    And yet we trust it comes from thee,
A beam in darkness: let it grow.

Let knowledge grow from more to more,
    But more of reverence in us dwell;
    That mind and soul, according well,
May make one music as before,

But vaster.  We are fools and slight;
    We mock thee when we do not fear:
    But help thy foolish ones to bear;
Help thy vain worlds to bear thy light.

Forgive what seem'd my sin in me;
    What seem'd my worth since I began;
    For merit lives from man to man,
And not from man, O Lord, to thee.

Forgive my grief for one removed,
    Thy creature, whom I found so fair,
    I trust he lives in thee, and there
I find him worthier to be loved.

Forgive these wild and wandering cries,
    Confusions of a wasted youth;
    Forgive them where they fail in truth,
And in thy wisdom make me wise.

### Darwin's "Origin of Species"

Tennyson's simple expressions of religious faith came not a moment too soon in the moral destiny of the nation, because after 1859 many of the basic Christian dogmas were to be questioned seriously in the light of Charles Darwin's theories on the evolution of life (in the *Origin of Species*).

Nevertheless, as has been pointed out in Romanes's *Darwin and after Darwin*, Tennyson had himself touched on the matter of Natural Selection ten years before the scientist—"In 'In Memoriam' Tennyson noted the fact, and a few years later Darwin supplied the explanations." Tennyson, like Darwin himself, believed that the theory of Evolution could be made compatible with Christianity, although many contended that it undermined the Old Testament.

Later, in 1868, when Darwin visited Farringford, the Poet, not yet entirely satisfied about it, asked the scientist if his theory of Evolution made against Christianity. Darwin's reply was, "No, certainly not." Yet many churchmen believed, and still believe, that it did.

However, the Poet's artistic interest and involvement in the latest developments of science, were like oil on troubled waters, and though oil and water are not compatible themselves, at least the tempest between Christianity and the theory of Evolution was temporarily quieted.

### Tennyson's Honeymoon
*In Memoriam* was a great success, but even with so propitious a start, Tennyson's work had only just begun. At last he had financial security, but he could not afford to rest on his laurels at this stage. He found happiness, too, and after his marriage to Emily, the couple travelled north to spend their honeymoon at Lake Coniston in a cottage lent to them by James Marshall.

The Poet recalled, with amusement, in a conversation with Arthur Coleridge in later years, how an American newspaper had reported the honeymoon: " 'We hope, now that Mr. Tennyson is married and has returned to his native lakes, that he will give up opium.' The penny-a-liners evidently confounded your uncle S. T. Coleridge, with myself,—anyhow if he wasn't quite certain, he gave your relative the benefit of the doubt."

### Browning and Swinburne
The couple also made a pilgrimage to Italy, the home of the Romantic exiles, and, on the return journey through Paris, met Browning, who with Swinburne and others, was to contribute a powerful influence on Victorian literature during the latter half of the nineteenth century.

### Isle of Wight visited
All that the Tennysons required now was a secluded house in attractive surroundings, where they could escape the hurly-burly of London's literary society, to work, dream and to raise a family to consummate their marriage. It is not certain if Tennyson were originally attracted to the Isle of Wight consciously by the memory of his beloved Keats, who had composed a large proportion of his poetry there, but it is more than likely. During his visit in 1852, however, he decided to rent a house at Freshwater, for his wife and baby boy, Hallam (named after A. H. Hallam) and in November of the following year they moved into Farringford.

**The View from Farringford**
"Next day," wrote Hallam Tennyson, in the *Memoir* of his father, "as they gazed from the drawing-room window out through the distant wreath of trees towards a sea of Mediterranean blue, with rosy capes beyond, the down on the left rising above the foreground of undulating park, golden-leaved elms and chestnuts, and red-stemmed pines, they agreed that they must, if possible, have that view to live with."   And they did for the greater part of forty years.

# POEMS DESCRIPTIVE OF FARRINGFORD

The following poem was sent to F. D. Maurice in January 1854. Maurice was then deeply involved, with Charles Kingsley and others, in the controversial Christian socialist movement, a breakaway much frowned on by the orthodox Church.

After Hallam Tennyson was born at Twickenham in 1852, Maurice was asked to be his godfather at the christening, which he gladly consented to do.

### TO THE REV. F. D. MAURICE

Come, when no graver cares employ,
Godfather, come and see your boy:
   Your presence will be sun in winter,
Making the little one leap for joy.

For, being of that honest few,
Who give the Fiend himself his due,
   Should eighty-thousand college-councils
Thunder "Anathema," friend, at you; (1)

Should all our churchmen foam in spite
At you, so careful of the right,
   Yet one lay-hearth would give you welcome
(Take it and come) to the Isle of Wight;

Where, far from noise and smoke of town,
I watch the twilight falling brown
   All round a careless-order'd garden
Close to the ridge of a noble down.

You'll have no scandal while you dine,
But honest talk and wholesome wine,
   And only hear the magpie gossip
Garrulous under a roof of pine:

For groves of pine on either hand,
To break the blast of winter, stand;
   And further on, the hoary Channel
Tumbles a breaker on chalk and sand;

Where, if below the milky steep
Some ship of battle slowly creep,
   And on thro' zones of light and shadow
Glimmer away to the lonely deep,

We might discuss the Northern sin
Which made a selfish war begin;
   Dispute the claims, arrange the chances;
Emperor, Ottoman, which shall win:

Or whether war's avenging rod
Shall lash all Europe into blood;
   Till you should turn to dearer matters,
Dear to the man that is dear to God;

How best to help the slender store,
How mend the dwellings, of the poor;
   How gain in life, as life advances,
Valour and charity more and more.

Come, Maurice, come: the lawn as yet
Is hoar with rime, or spongy-wet;
   But when the wreath of March has blossom'd,
Crocus, anemone, violet,

Or later, pay one visit here,
For those are few we hold as dear;
   Nor pay but one, but come for many,
Many and many a happy year.

(1) Maurice, who was professor of English Literature and History at King's College, London, for thirteen years, was dismissed from his post in 1853, because of his views on Eternal Punishment.

    . . . . .

The poem *To Gifford Palgrave* was composed in 1888. Gifford was the brother of Tennyson's devoted friend, Francis T. Palgrave, who compiled the famous "Golden Treasury." In his

Preface to the first edition (May 1861), F. T. Palgrave acknowledges Tennyson's invaluable advice and assistance: "Your encouragement, given while traversing the wild scenery of Treryn Dinas, led me to begin the work; and it has been completed under your advice and assistance. For the favour now asked I have thus a second reason: and to this I may add, the homage which is your right as Poet, and the gratitude due to a Friend, whose regard I rate at no common value."

*Ulysses*, mentioned in the first stanza, refers to a volume of essays of that title, by W. G. Palgrave. "Or watch the waving pine which here / the warrior of Caprera set," speaks of a Wellingtonia pine planted by Garibaldi opposite the house, during the latter's visit to Farringford in 1864. The tree is now all of eighty feet high.

## TO GIFFORD PALGRAVE

Ulysses, much-experienced man,
    Whose eyes have known this globe of ours,
    Her tribes of men, and trees, and flowers,
From Corrientes to Japan,

To you that bask below the Line,
    I soaking here in winter wet—
    The century's three strong eights have met
To drag me down to seventy-nine

In summer if I reach my day—
    To you, yet young, who breathe the balm
    Of summer-winters by the palm
And orange grove of Paraguay,

I tolerant of the colder time,
    Who love the winter woods, to trace
    On paler heavens the branching grace
Of leafless elm, or naked lime,

And see my cedar green, and there
    My giant ilex keeping leaf
    When frost is keen and days are brief—
Or marvel how in English air

My yucca, which no winter quells,
   Altho' the months have scarce begun,
   Has push'd toward our faintest sun
A spike of half-accomplish'd bells—

Or watch the waving pine which here
   The warrior of Caprera set,
   A name that earth will not forget
Till earth has roll'd her latest year—

I, once half-crazed for larger light
   On broader zones beyond the foam,
   But chaining fancy now at home
Among the quarried downs of Wight,

Not less would yield full thanks to you
   For your rich gift, your tale of lands
   I know not, your Arabian sands;
Your cane, your palm, tree-fern, bamboo,

The wealth of tropic bower and brake;
   Your Oriental Eden-isles,
   Where man, nor only Nature smiles;
Your wonder of the boiling lake;

Phra-Chai, the Shadow of the Best,
   Phra-bat the step; your Pontic coast;
   Crag-cloister; Anatolian Ghost;
Hong-Kong, Karnac, and all the rest.

Thro' which I follow'd line by line
   Your leading hand, and came, my friend,
   To prize your various book, and send
A gift of slenderer value, mine.

. . . . .

# I HAVE LED HER HOME,
# MY LOVE

THE Tennysons fell in love at first sight with the secluded, late Georgian house—with its Gothic-style windows and castellated walls—that nestled so romantically among the ancient trees and undulating meadows. To the south the magnificently swelling green slopes of High Down (now Tennyson Down) were an open invitation to walk, an invitation the Poet rarely refused on his daily rounds. To seaward the down fell away precipitously for hundreds of feet in a "milky steep" of chalk cliffs, and its extremities were at the Needles and at Freshwater Bay, where the sound of the sea on the shingly beach was a "broad-flung ship-wrecking roar." The Poet felt he had no choice but to rent Farringford from the Seymours, with the option to buy later.

The early records of the estate go back to the fourteenth century, and the name of one witness, Walter de Ferringford, appears most frequently on the title deeds. The present house stands near the site of the original Prior's Manor, which then belonged to the Abbey of Lyra in Normandy. The farmland adjacent (part of the estate in Tennyson's day), was of nearly three hundred acres, and included fields retaining their original names—Prior's Field, Maiden's Croft (dedicated to the Virgin Mary), the Clerk's Hill (where the Clerk of the Monastery lived), St. George (where the archers shot) and Abraham's Mead.

Though the Poet had invested in safe Railway debentures and had been earning £500 annually from his books since 1850, he as yet could not afford to buy the estate outright. The opportunity to do so came one spring three years later, as a result of an intimate friendship with Sir John Simeon of Swainston, near Calbourne.

Lionel, the Poet's second son, was born in 1854, and Sir John visited Farringford after the christening. He found "the family party just returning from church," recalls Mrs. Richard Ward (Sir John's eldest daughter). "During these early years, it was one of my father's greatest pleasures to ride or drive over from Swainston in the summer afternoons. He and the Tennysons would go long expeditions through the lanes and over the downs: then back through the soft evening air to dinner and to the long evening of talk and of reading, which knit 'that fair companionship' and made it 'such a friendship as had mastered time'."

**Simeon and "Maud"**
Sir John, during one of his frequent visits to Farringford, had seen these four lines of verse among the Poet's papers in his study:

> O that 'twere possible
> After long grief and pain
> To find the arms of my true love
> Round me once again!

He was immediately struck with their simple beauty and pathos, and begged the Poet to incorporate them in a much longer poem, and in this way the poem *Maud* came into being.

**Composed Backwards**
The composition of the poem, *Maud*, was done in a most unusual manner. It was written from the middle, backwards. Aubrey de Vere describes the accidental process: "He (Tennyson) had ... lighted upon a poem of his own which begins, 'O that 'twere possible,' and which had long before been published in a selected volume got up by Lord Northampton for the aid of a sick clergyman. It had struck him, in consequence, I think, of a suggestion made by Sir John Simeon, that, to render the poem intelligible, a preceding one was necessary"—

> Courage, poor heart of stone!
> I will not ask thee why
> Thou canst not understand
> That thou art left for ever alone:
> Courage, poor stupid heart of stone.
> Or if I ask thee why,
> Care not thou to reply:
> She is but dead, and the time is at hand
> When thou shalt more than die.

"He wrote it; the second poem too required a predecessor"—

> Who knows if he be dead?
> Whether I need have fled?
> Am I guilty of blood?
> However this may be,
> Comfort her, comfort her, all things good,
> While I am over the sea!
> Let me and my passionate love go by,
> But speak to her all things holy and high,
> Whatever happen to me!
> Me and my harmful love go by;
> But come to her waking, find her asleep,
> Powers of the height, Powers of the deep,
> And comfort her tho' I die.—

"and thus the whole work was written, as it were, *backwards*."

Tennyson worked on the poem morning and evening, "sitting in his hard high-backed wooden chair in his little room at the top of the house," wrote Hallam in his *Memoir*. "His 'sacred pipes,' as he called them, were half an hour after breakfast, and half an hour after dinner, when no one was allowed to be with him, for then his best thoughts came to him. As he made the different poems he would repeat or read them. The constant reading of the new poems aloud was the surest way of helping him to find out any defects there might be. During the 'sacred half-hours' and his other working hours and even on the Downs, he would murmur his new passages or new lines as they came to him, a habit which had always been his since boyhood, and which caused the Somersby cook to say 'What is master Awlfred always a praying for ?' "

## Maud's Poor Reception

When the poem appeared in 1855, it was generally misunderstood, even by men of Gladstone's intellectual calibre who should have shown keener critical perception. But a time came when Gladstone recanted publicly on what he had at first said of it.

A few like the Brownings, Jowett and Henry Taylor, however) were enthusiastic from the beginning in praise of the poem. However, to prevent any future misinterpretation of the work, the Poet asked Hallam, his son, to publish in his *Memoir*, the following explanatory notes on *Maud*:

## PART I
*Sections*
- I. Before the arrival of Maud.
- II. First sight of Maud.
- III. Visions of the night. The broad-flung ship wrecking roar. In the Isle of Wight the roar can be heard nine miles away from the beach. (Many of the descriptions of Nature are taken from observations of natural phenomena at Farringford, although the localities in the poem are all imaginary.)
- IV. Mood of bitterness after fancied disdain.
- V. He fights against his growing passion.
- VI. First interview with Maud.
- VII. He remembers his own and her father talking just before the birth of Maud.
- VIII. That she did not return his love.
- IX. First sight of the young lord.
- X. The *Westminster Review* said this was an attack on John Bright. I did not know at the time that he was a Quaker. (It was not against Quakers but against peace-at-all-price men that the hero fulminates.)
- XI. This was originally verse III, but I omitted it.

> Will she smile if he presses her hand,
> This lord-captain up at the Hall?
> Captain! he to hold a command!
> He can hold a cue, he can pocket a ball;
> And sure not a bantam cockerel lives
> With a weaker crow upon English land,
> Whether he boast of a horse that gains,
> Or cackle his own applause....
>
> What use for a single mouth to rage
> At the rotten creak of the State-machine;
> Tho' it makes friends weep and enemies smile,
> That here in the face of a watchful age,
> The sons of a gray-beard-ridden isle
> Should dance in a round of an old routine.

- XII. Interview with Maud.
    "Maud, Maud, Maud" is like the rook's caw.
    "Maud is here, here, here" is like the call of the little birds.
- XIII. Mainly prophetic. He sees Maud's brother who will not recognize him.
- XVI. He will declare his love.
- XVII. Accepted.
- XVIII. Happy. The sigh in the cedar branches seems to chime in with his own yearning.
    "*Sad astrology*" is modern astronomy, for of old astrology was thought to sympathize with and rule man's fate. *Not die but live a life of truest breath*. This is the central idea, the holy power of Love.
- XXI. Before the Ball.
- XXII. In the Hall-Garden.

## PART II

*Sections*
- I. The Phantom (after the duel with Maud's brother).
- II. In Brittany. The shell undestroyed amid the storm perhaps symbolizes to him his own first and highest nature preserved amid the storms of passion.
- III. He felt himself going mad.
- IV. Haunted after Maud's death.
    "O that 'twere possible" appeared first in the *Tribute*. Sir John Simeon years after begged me to weave a story round this poem and so "Maud" came into being.
- V. In the mad-house.
    The second corpse is Maud's brother, the lover's father being the first corpse, whom the lover thinks that Maud's father has murdered.

## PART III

- VI. Sane but shattered. Written when the cannon was heard booming from the battleships in the Solent before the Crimean War.

## "Maud" Pays for Farringford

Although there were many adverse criticisms of *Maud*, the poem sold quite well, and with the proceeds Tennyson was at last able to buy Farringford. On April 30th, 1856, Mrs. Tennyson wrote happily in her journal:

"We have agreed to buy, so I suppose this ivied home among the pine-trees is ours. Went to our withy holt; such beautiful blue hyacinths, orchises, primroses, daisies, marsh-marigolds and cuckoo-flowers. Wild cherry trees too with single snowy blossom. and the hawthorns white with their 'pearls of May.' The park has for many days been rich with cowslips and furze in bloom. The elms are a golden wreath at the foot of the Down; to the north of the house the mespilus and horse-chestnut are in flower and the apple-trees are covered with rosy buds. A. [Alfred] dug the bed ready for the rhododendrons. A thrush was singing among the nightingales and other birds, as he said 'mad with joy.' At sunset, the golden green of the trees, the burning splendour of Blackgang Chine and St. Catherine's, and the red bank of the primeval river, contrasted with the turkis-blue of the sea (that is our view from the drawing-room), make altogether a miracle of beauty. We are glad that Farringford is ours."

## The Poet's Favourite

Of all his poems, *Maud* was perhaps dearest to the Poet's heart, and he would not allow his friends to run it down within his hearing. Moreover, he beseeched them as well to defend his pet against all adverse comment. This affection for the work devolved, no doubt, from its sweet associations with Farringford and Sir John Simeon of Swainston.

The three passages he favoured most were the two already quoted— "O that 'twere possible" and "Courage, poor heart of stone" — and that from Section XVIII, Part I:

### I.

I have led her home, my love, my only friend.
There is none like her, none.
And never yet so warmly ran my blood
And sweetly, on and on
Calming itself to the long-wish'd-for end,
Full to the banks, close on the promised good.

## II.

None like her, none.
Just now the dry-tongued laurels' pattering talk (1)
Seem'd her light foot along the garden walk
And shook my heart to think she comes once more;
But even then I heard her close the door,
The gates of Heaven are closed, and she is gone.

## III.

There is none like her, none.
Nor will be when our summers have deceased.
O, art thou sighing for Lebanon
In the long breeze that streams to thy delicious East,
Sighing for Lebanon,
Dark cedar, tho' thy limbs have here increased,
Upon a pastoral slope as fair,
And looking to the South, and fed
With honey'd rain and delicate air,
And haunted by the starry head
Of her whose gentle will has changed my fate,
And made my life a perfumed alter-flame;
And over whom thy darkness must have spread
With such delight as theirs of old, thy great
Forefathers of the thornless garden, there
Shadowing the snow-limb'd Eve from whom she came.

## IV.

Here will I lie, while these long branches sway,
And you fair stars that crown a happy day
Go in and out as if at merry play,
Who am no more so all forlorn,
As when it seem'd far better to be born
To labour and the mattock-harden'd hand,
Than nursed at ease and brought to understand
A sad astrology, the boundless plan (2)
That makes you tyrants in your iron skies,
Innumerable, pitiless, passionless eyes,
Cold fires, yet with power to burn and brand
His nothingness into man.

### V.

But now shine on, and what care I,
Who in this stormy gulf have found a pearl
The countercharm of space and hollow sky,
And do accept my madness, and would die
To save from some slight shame one simple girl.

### VI.

Would die; for sullen-seeming Death may give
More life to Love than is or ever was
In our low world, where yet 'tis sweet to live.
Let no one ask me how it came to pass;
It seems that I am happy, that to me
A livelier emerald twinkles in the grass,
A purer sapphire melts into the sea.

### VII.

Not die; but live a life of truest breath,
And teach true life to fight with mortal wrongs.
O, why should Love, like men in drinking-songs,
Spice his fair banquet with the dust of death?
Make answer, Maud my bliss,
Maud made my Maud by that long lover's kiss,
Life of my life, wilt thou not answer this?
"The dusky strand of Death inwoven here
With dear Love's tie, makes Love himself more dear."

### VIII.

Is that enchanted moan only the swell
Of the long waves that roll in yonder bay?
And hark the clock within, the silver knell
Of twelve sweet hours that past in bridal white,
And died to live, long as my pulses play;
But now by this my love has closed her sight
And given false death her hand, and stol'n away
To dreamful wastes where footless fancies dwell
Among the fragments of the golden day.
May nothing there her maiden grace affright!
Dear heart, I feel with thee the drowsy spell.
My bride to be, my evermore delight,
My own heart's heart and ownest own, farewell;
It is but for a little space I go:

And ye meanwhile far over moor and fell
Beat to the noiseless music of the night!
Has our whole earth gone nearer to the glow
Of your soft splendours that you look so bright?
I have climb'd nearer out of lonely Hell.
Beat, happy stars, timing with things below,
Beat with my heart more blest than heart can tell,
Blest, but for some dark undercurrent woe
That seems to draw-but it shall not be so:
Let all be well, be well.

(1) "The dry-tongued laurels' pattering talk," describes exactly the sound of laurel leaves flapping together as they are stirred by a summer's breeze. There were laurels in the grounds of Farringford.

(2) The Poet's up-to-date pastimes included geology, botany, bird-watching and astronomy. At night he studied the stars through a telescope from the roof of the house.

## The Prince of Courtesy

During his lifetime, Tennyson loved three men more dearly than any other. These were Arthur Henry Hallam, Harry Lushington and Sir John Simeon. The Poet outlived them all by many years. Sir John, the last of these friends to go, has been described as "a tall, broad-shouldered, genial, generous, warm-hearted, highly-gifted, and thoroughly noble country gentleman; in face like the portrait of Sir Thomas Wyatt, by Holbein."

Tennyson looked upon him as a brother, and when the news came of Sir John's death at Friburg, on March 23rd, 1870, it was a terrible blow, not only to the Poet, but also to his family. On the 31st, the Poet attended the funeral at Swainston, and while the coffin lay in the house, he took one of his friend's pipes with him to smoke in the garden, and there, beneath a cedar, he wrote these lines *To Sir John Simeon*:

## IN THE GARDEN OF SWAINSTON

Nightingales warbled without,
    Within was weeping for thee:
Shadows of three dead men
    Walk'd in the walks with me,
Shadows of three dead men and thou wast
    one of the three.

Nightingales sang in his woods:
    The Master was far away:
Nightingales warbled and sang
    Of a passion that lasts but a day;
Still in the house in his coffin the Prince
    of courtesy lay.

Two dead men have I known
    In courtesy like to thee:
Two dead men have I loved
    With a love that ever will be:
Three dead men have I loved and thou art
    last of the three.

# GOD-GIFTED ORGAN-VOICE OF ENGLAND

The phrase "God-gifted organ-voice of England," was used by Tennyson of the poet, Milton, England's mouthpiece in the seventeenth century. It could equally well have been said of himself as Poet Laureate in the second half of the nineteenth century.

God-gifted, indeed, was this born Poet, and his organ-voice was soon, in 1852, to reverberate throughout the nation, rousing the hearts of Englishmen everywhere, expressing their innermost fears of the French—

> We love not this French God, the child of Hell,
>   Wild War, who breaks the converse of the wise;
> But though we love kind Peace so well,
>   We dare not ev'n by silence sanction lies.—

enjoining them, here, to

> ... Curse the crimes of southern kings,
> The Russian whips and Austrian rods,

or, there, to lament the death of the great Duke of Wellington—

> Bury the Great Duke
>   With an empire's lamentation,
> Let us bury the Great Duke
>   To the noise of the mourning of a mighty nation,
> Mourning when their leaders fall,
> Warriors carry the warrior's pall,
> And sorrow darkens hamlet and hall.

His voice was the voice of England. It spoke from the heart of the nation, expressing completely its sentiments of determined patriotism. Tennyson, like his fellow-countrymen, did not want war. He abhorred war, the horror of it, the death and destruction that followed inevitably in its wake, but how long must one submit to tyranny without retaliating. No longer in 1852, he felt,

> Tho' all men else their nobler dreams forget,
> Confused by brainless mobs and lawless Powers.

### Death of the Duke of Wellington

Some critics like Stopford Brooke, however, believed that Tennyson over-reached the bounds of his poetic duties on occasion, as in Section VII of the *Ode on the Death of the Duke of Wellington*. He felt the Poet was too patriotic, too exclusively English, too controversial, made too much an attack on France. Moreover, he was "too contemptuous of the people whom he sees only as a mob; too fond of the force of great men to the exclusion of the force of the collective movements of the nation. A great artist should not overstep so much the limits of temperance; or, to put it otherwise, he should not lose his sympathy with the whole of humanity in his sympathy with his own country."

But, with a few reservations, such as the over-playing of the Duke's virtues as against his weaknesses, this ode was seen to be a great work of art. "The metrical movement rushes on where it ought to rush, delays where it ought to delay. Were the poem see by Handel, its rhythmical movements could scarcely be more fit from point to point to the things spoken of, more full of stately, happy changes." (Stopford Brooke)

In Section VI, the swelling harmony and growing thought reaches its climax when the spirit of Nelson, that "Mighty Seaman," asks from his grave,

> Who is he that cometh, like an honour'd guest,
> With banner and with music, with soldier and with priest,
> With a nation weeping, and breaking on my rest?

The Poet assures him that

> ... this is he
> Was great by land as thou by sea ....
> Now, to the roll of muffled drums,
> To thee the greatest soldier comes ....

Be glad, because his bones are laid by thine!
And thro' the centuries let a people's voice
In full acclaim,
A people's voice,
The proof and echo of all human fame,
A people's voice, when they rejoice
At civic revel and pomp and game,
Attest their great commander's claim
With honour, honour, honour, honour to him
Eternal honour to his name.

## The Charge of the Light Brigade

Popular as was the *Ode to the Duke of Wellington*, it never received the wide-spread acclaim, however less deserved, of *The Charge of the Light Brigade*, which was inspired by a tragic incident in the Crimea War, in 1854.

One morning the Poet, who was now at Farringford, read an account of the charge of the Light Brigade at Balaclava. The phrase— "some one had blundered"—formed itself in his mind as he set out for his usual walk over High Down. The rhythm of the words became that of the whole poem, and the lines came easily to him:

### THE CHARGE OF THE LIGHT BRIGADE

Half a league, half a league,
  Half a league onward,
All in the valley of Death
  Rode the six hundred.
"Forward, the Light Brigade!
  Charge for the guns!" he said;
Into the valley of Death
  Rode the six hundred.

"Forward, the Light Brigade!"
Was there a man dismay'd?
Not tho' the soldier knew
  Some one had blunder'd:
Their's not to make reply,
Their's not to reason why,
Their's but to do and die:
Into the valley of Death
  Rode the six hundred.

Cannon to right of them,
Cannon to left of them,
Cannon in front of them
   Volley'd and thunder'd;
Storm'd at with shot and shell,
Boldly they rode and well,
Into the jaws of Death,
Into the mouth of Hell
   Rode the six hundred.

Flash'd all their sabres bare,
Flash'd as they turn'd in air,
Sabring the gunners there,
Charging an army, while
   All the world wonder'd:
Plunged in the battery-smoke
Right thro' the line they broke;
Cossack and Russian
Reel'd from the sabre-stroke
   Shatter'd and sunder'd.
Then they rode back, but not,
   Not the six hundred.

Cannon to right of them,
Cannon to left of them,
Cannon behind them
   Volley'd and thunder'd;
Storm'd at with shot and shell,
While horse and hero fell,
They that had fought so well
Came thro' the jaws of Death
Back from the mouth of Hell,
All that was left of them
   Left of six hundred.

When can their glory fade?
O the wild charge they made!
   All the world wonder'd.
Honour the charge they made
Honour the Light Brigade,
   Noble six hundred!

The poem was published in *The Examiner* on December 9th,

1854. On August 6th, 1855, Tennyson wrote: "'The Balaclava Charge' with the following short preface was forwarded to John Forster to be printed on a fly-leaf for the Crimean Soldiers.

August 8th, 1855.

"Having heard that the brave soldiers before Sebastopol, whom I am proud to call my countrymen, having a liking for my ballad on the charge of the Light Brigade at Balaclava, I have ordered a thousand copies of it to be printed for them. No writing of mine can add to the glory they have acquired in the Crimea; but if what I have heard be true, they will not be displeased to receive these copies from me, and to know that those who sit at home love and honour them."

The Poet later received the following tribute from Scutari: "We had in hospital a man of the Light Brigade, one of the few who survived that fatal mistake, the Balaclava charge; but which, deplorable as it was, at least tended to show the high state of discipline attained in the British Army. I spoke to several of those engaged in that deadly conflict, and they could describe accurately the position of the Russian cannon; were perfectly aware when obeying that word of command, that they rode to almost certain death. This patient had received a kick in the chest from a horse long after the battle of Balaclava, while in barracks at Scutari. He was depressed in spirits, which prevented him from throwing off the disease engendered by the blow. The doctor remarked that he wished the soldier could be roused. Amongst other remedies leeches was prescribed. While watching them I tried to enter into a conversation with him, spoke of the charge, but could elicit only monosyllabic replies. A copy of Tennyson's poem having been lent to me that morning, I took it out and read it. The man, with kindling eye, at once entered upon a spirited description of the fatal gallop between the guns' mouths to and from that cannon-crowded height. He asked to hear it again, but, as by this time a number of convalescents were gathered around, I slipped out of the ward. The chaplain who had lent me the poem, understanding the enthusiasm with which it had been received, afterwards procured from England a number of copies for distribution. In a few days the invalid requested the doctor to discharge him for duty, being now in health; but whether the cure was effected by the leeches or the poem it is impossible to say. On giving the card the medical man murmured, 'Well done, Tennyson!' "

# MY OWN IDEAL KNIGHT

When Farringford became his in 1856, Tennyson sent for the family's goods and chattels from Twickenham, where they had been stored. Very soon the ground-floor rooms were "in wild disarray." Piles of books, too, littered the drawing-room floor, and if there were one thing they least desired then it was the arrival of visitors.

But, inevitably, as it would happen, a loud rap was heard at the front door, and in a state of near panic, the parlour-maid answered it. It is not difficult to imagine her utter confusion of mind, on opening the door, to find herself face to face with Prince Albert, the Queen's Consort, who had just driven over from Osborne House.

Here Hallam Tennyson takes up the story: "Being bewildered and not knowing into what room to show him, [she] stood stock still; so the Equerry, I have been told, took her by the shoulders and turned her round, bidding her lead them in."

The Prince, however, seeming not to notice the disorder in the drawing-room, expressed great admiration of the view of the downs, of Freshwater Bay and the distant cliffs. And seeing cowslips in the garden, he sent one of his party to gather a bunch for the Queen.

Tennyson found the Prince to be very cordial, and he impressed him as being a man of strong and self-sacrificing nature. Over the years a sincere respect grew and strengthened between them. The Prince himself admired the Poet and his work, especially the Arthurian legends. In Royal circles the Prince was often linked with the idea of the legendary King.

**"Idylls of the King"**
For many years the Poet regarded the writing of the Idylls as the fulfilment of his life's work, his *magnum opus*, by which he would prefer posterity to remember him. His first essays on the

Arthurian theme, as in *The Lady of Shalott, Galahad* and *Morte d'Arthur*, had been purely romantic in treatment, but the later Idylls, published in 1859, were allegories representing King Arthur as "the Ideal in the Soul of Man coming in contact with the warring elements of the flesh." These showed the different ways in which men regard Conscience, "some reverencing it as a heaven-born king, others ascribing to it an earthly origin."

Hallam Tennyson explains that his father "has made the old legends his own, restored the idealism, and infused into them a spirit of modern thought and of ethical significance; setting his characters in a rich and varied landscape; as indeed otherwise these archaic stories would not have appealed to the world at large."

However, this attempt, in the Idylls, to teach an old dog new tricks, so to speak, to cast an ancient and essentially mythical King as a modern-day ethical preacher—however beautifully disguised— was an inescapable weakness in the eyes of some Victorian realists. "Not everyone," Sir Alfred Lyall points out, "has been able to overcome the effect of incongruity produced by a poem which invests the legendary personages of mediaeval romance with morals and manners of a fastidious delicacy, and promotes them to the embodiment of our own ethical ideals."

There was wide admiration for Tennyson's earlier interpretations of the Arthurian legends on both sides of the Atlantic, and some preferred them to the later allegories. In 1854 H. W. Longfellow wrote to J. T. Fields: "The *Idylls* . . . are a brilliant success. Rich tapestries wrought as only Tennyson could have done them, and worthy to hang by the *Faerie Queene*. I believe there is no discordant voice on this side of the water."

**Idyll of Guinevere Read**
Another American, Bayard Taylor, once had the enviable and moving experience of hearing the Poet recite *Guinevere* at Farringford.

"I spoke of the Idyll of Guinevere as being perhaps his finest poem, and said that I could not read it aloud without my voice breaking down at certain passages. 'Why, I can read it and keep my voice,' he [Tennyson] exclaimed triumphantly. This I doubted, and he agreed to try. Afterwards we went down to our wives. But the first thing he did was to produce a magnum of sherry . . . .

"We had two glasses apiece, when he said, 'Tonight you shall help me drink one of the few bottles of my Waterloo—1815.' The bottle was brought, and after another glass all round, Tennyson took up the *Idylls of the King*. His reading is a strange, monotonous chant, with unexpected falling inflexions, which I cannot describe, but can imitate exactly. It was very impressive. In spite of myself I became very much excited as he went on. Finally, when Arthur forgives the Queen, Tennyson's voice broke. I found tears on his cheeks, and Mr. and Mrs. Tennyson were crying, one on either side of me. He made an effort and went on to the end, closing grandly.

" 'How can you say,' I asked [referring to a previous conversation], 'that you have no surety of permanent fame? This poem will only die with the language in which it is written.' Mrs. Tennyson started up from her couch, 'It is true!' she exclaimed, 'I have told Alfred the same thing.' "

Here is the moving passage from *Guinevere*, in which Arthur forgives the Queen her unfaithfulness:

## FROM **GUINEVERE**

"Yet think not that I am come to urge thy crimes,
I did not come to curse thee, Guinevere,
I, whose vast pity almost makes me die
To see thee, laying there thy golden head,
My pride in happier summers, at my feet.
The wrath which forced my thoughts on that fierce law,
The doom of treason and the flaming death,
(When first I learnt thee hidden here) is past.
The pang—which while I weigh'd thy heart with one
Too wholly true to dream untruth in thee,
Made my tears burn—is also past, in part.
And all is past, the sin is sinn'd, and I,
Lo! I forgive thee, as Eternal God
Forgives: do thou for thine own soul the rest.
But how to take last leave of all I loved?
O golden hair, with which I used to play
Not knowing! O imperial-moulded form,

Arid beauty such as never woman wore,
Until it came a kingdom's curse with thee—
I cannot touch thy lips, they are not mine,
But Lancelot's: nay, they never were the King's.
I cannot take thy hand; that too is flesh,
And in the flesh thou hast sinn'd; and mine own flesh,
Here looking down on thine polluted, cries
'I loathe thee:' yet not less, O Guinevere,
For I was ever virgin save for thee,
My love thro' flesh hath wrought into my life
So far, that my doom is, I love thee still.
Let no man dream but that I love thee still.
Perchance, and so thou purify thy soul,
And so thou lean on our fair father Christ,
Hereafter in that world where all are pure
We two may meet before high God, and thou
Wilt spring to me, and claim me thine, and know
I am thine husband—not a smaller soul,
Nor Lancelot, nor another. Leave me that,
I charge thee, my last hope. Now must I hence.
Thro' the thick night I hear the trumpet blow:
They summon me their King to lead mine hosts
Far down to that great battle in the west,
Where I must strike against my sister's son,
Leagued with the lords of the White Horse and knights
Once mine, and strike him dead, and meet myself
Death, or I know not what mysterious doom.
And thou remaining here wilt learn the event;
But hither shall I never come again,
Never lie by thy side, see thee no more:
Farewell!"
              And while she grovell'd at his feet,
She felt the King's breath wander o'er her neck,
And, in the darkness o'er her fallen head,
Perceiving the waving of his hands that blest.

## Death of the Prince

On February 23rd, 1862, the Crown Princess of Prussia wrote the following letter to the Poet (Prince Albert had died in December of the previous year):

"The first time I ever heard the *Idylls of the King* was last year, when I found both the Queen and Prince quite in raptures about them. The first bit I ever heard was the end of *Guinevere*, the last two or three pages: the Prince read them to me, and I shall never forget the impression it made upon me hearing those grand and simple words in his voice! He did so admire them, and I cannot separate the idea of King Arthur from the image of him whom I most revered on earth!

"I almost know the *Idylls of the King* by heart now: they are really sublime!

"Surely it must give the Author satisfaction to think that his words have been drops of balm on the broken and loving hearts of the widowed Queen and her orphaned children."

**The Dedication**
The *Dedication* to the late lamented Prince Albert, was included in the 1862 edition of the Idylls, and a copy was sent to the Queen:

### DEDICATION
(From the **Idylls of the King,** 1862)

These to His Memory—since he held them dear,
Perchance as finding there unconsciously
Some image of himself—I dedicate,
I dedicate, I consecrate with tears—
These Idylls.

                And indeed He seems to me
Scarce other than my own ideal knight,
"Who reverenced his conscience as his king;
Whose glory was, redressing human wrong;
Who spake no slander, no, nor listen'd to it;
Who loved one only and who clave to her—"
Her—over all whose realms to their last isle,
Commingled with the gloom of imminent war,
The shadow of His loss drew like eclipse,
Darkening the world. We have lost him: he is gone:
We know him now: all narrow jealousies
Are silent; and we see him as he moved,
How modest, kindly, all-accomplish'd, wise,
With what sublime repression of himself,
And in what limits, and how tenderly;

Not swaying to this faction or to that;
Not making his high place the lawless perch
Of wing'd ambitions, nor a vantage-ground
For pleasure; but thro' all this tract of years
Wearing the white flower of a blameless life,
Before a thousand peering littlenesses,
In that fierce light which beats upon a throne,
And blackens every blot: for where is he,
Who dares foreshadow for an only son
A lovelier life, a more unstain'd, than his?
Or how should England dreaming of *his* sons
Hope more for these than some inheritance
Of such a life, a heart, a mind as thine,
Thou noble Father of her Kings to be,
Laborious for her people and her poor—
Voice in the rich dawn of an ampler day—
Far-sighted summoner of War and Waste
To fruitful strifes and rivalries of peace—
Sweet nature gilded by the gracious gleam
Of letters, dear to Science, dear to Art,
Dear to thy land and ours, a Prince indeed,
Beyond all titles, and a household name,
Hereafter, thro' all times, Albert the Good.

Break not, O woman's-heart, but still endure;
Break not, for thou art Royal, but endure,
Remembering all the beauty of that star
Which shone so close beside Thee, that ye made
One light together, but has past and leaves
The Crown a lonely splendour.

                                        May all love,
His love, unseen but felt, o'ershadow Thee,
The love of all Thy sons encompass Thee,
The love of all Thy daughters cherish Thee,
The love of all Thy people comfort Thee,
Till God's love set Thee at his side again!

(See page 81 for an extract from *The Passing of Arthur*,
first published December, 1869.)

Alfred, Lord Tennyson 1888

*Photograph by William Barraud*

Farringford

*Photograph by the author*

The newly restored terrace at Aldworth, Haslemere

*Photograph by Elizabeth Hutchings 1997*
*By kind permission of M.F. Keeley*

A corner of Tennyson's Study at Farringford
with the Poet's Deerhound Lufra and the Terrier Winks

*From a drawing by W. Biscombe Gardener*

The Summerhouse at Farringford
Carved and Painted by Tennyson. Enoch Arden written here.

*From a drawing by W. Biscombe Gardener*

The Laureate with his sons Hallam and Lionel

*Photograph by Julia Margaret Cameron*

**Freshwater Cave,** which Tennyson may have had in mind when composing *Enoch Arden*:
"A narrow cave ran in beneath the cliff:
In this the children play'd at keeping house."

*From Barber's Isle of Wight*

Freshwater Bay
Left to right; Fort Redoubt, Plumbleys
(now Freshwater Bay House. Holiday Fellowship Hotel), The Albion Hotel

*Photograph by Julia Margaret Cameron*

Freshwater Bay
Left to right; The Bath House, run by the Cotton family, where hot
sea water baths cost 6d. Destroyed during WW2; The Albion Hotel;
Glenbrook-St. Francis, May, Lady Tennyson's Religious Library run with the
help of Hester Thackeray Fuller and Alan May
(now re-built as apartments and named Tennyson's View).

*An original Watercolour by Sir Muirhead Bone 1920*
*By kind permission of Mrs. Belinda Norman - Butler*

The Drive at Farringford, showing on the left the
Wellingtonia planted by Garibaldi in 1867.

*From a drawing by W. Biscombe Gardener*

Mark, Lord Tennyson [1920-2006] unveiling the plaque Commemorating the
Centenary of Emily Tennyson's death, beside the Wellingtonia planted in 1996
by The Farringford Tennyson Society.

*Photograph by Elizabeth Hutchings 1997*

**In Memory of
Alfred Lord Tennyson
This is raised
a beacon to Sailors
by the people of
Freshwater and
other Friends
in England and America**

*August 6th. 1897*

The Tennyson Memorial
handed over to
Trinity House in the
presence of the
Archbishop of Canterbury
and a large crowd on
the anniversary of the
Laureate's birthday.

*Photograph by
the author 1963*

# THE SEA FROM MAIDEN'S CROFT

AT THE back of Farringford, a shaded lane between steep banks separates the grounds from the farm, and over this lane the Poet built himself a wooden bridge (extant) which leads into the "middle walk, bordered on either side with lilac-flowered aubretia." (E.V.B.)

This grove is between the lane and Maiden's Croft, and half way along it (facing Maiden's Croft), Tennyson, in 1858, constructed a summer-house with views of High Down opposite and Freshwater Bay to the south-east. On its windows he painted dragons and sea-serpents, and here and there he carved fanciful designs in the woodwork.

The little summer-house caught the southern sun, and many times he brought his friends here to enjoy the solitude. Here, too, he sat alone, or paced up and down the meadow, his imagination winging in passionate communion with Nature. The sound of the sea was often in his ears (I have personally stood near the site of the summer-house on one or two occasions, and have heard the scream of the shingle at Freshwater Bay as it is dragged down by the waves), and one day in 1864 he began work on rather a tragic poem called *Enoch Arden*, whose theme has been repeated in different guises ever since mariners first sailed the seven seas.

It speaks of the loves of the two boys, Philip Ray, the miller's only son, and Enoch Arden, a rough orphaned sailor's lad, for Annie. Turn and turn about, they play at being Annie's wife, in the cave under the cliff (there is such a cave under the chalk cliff at Freshwater Bay), and when eventually they grow up, it is Enoch who marries her.

They live happily together. A girl and then a boy is born to them, but Enoch, who soon owns a merchant vessel, spends long periods away from home. But while working in a neighbouring port, he breaks a limb, and during his enforced idleness the family becomes impoverished. And to make matters worse another child, a sickly one, is born. Then Enoch is offered employment as a boatswain on a China-bound trader, and Annie is talked into running a store much against her will. As Enoch sails away to make a fortune, Annie knows in her heart she will never see him again. She, living a "life of silent melancholy," finds she is not cut out to trade and barter. The store proves unsuccessful; she neglects her children and herself, and soon the baby dies. Philip Ray, now a prosperous miller, sees the plight of Annie and her children, and offers friendship and financial help. The children grow to love him as a father, but Annie remains faithful to Enoch for more than ten years. But when there no longer seems any hope for his return, she marries Philip and they have a child of their own. During the years of absence, Enoch has become a wealthy trader, and when returning home his vessel is shipwrecked. His two surviving companions die, and he is left alone on an uninhabited shore. Time drags intolerably, and "waiting for a sail," he dreams of home, of Annie and the babes, convinced he will never see them again.

Eventually he, a prematurely aged and broken man, is rescued and brought home, and

> He like a lover down thro' all his blood
> Drew in the dewy meadowy morning-breath
> Of England....

Enoch learns from Miriam Lane, who keeps the harbour tavern, that his wife has married Philip. Despair and grief overwhelm him, but he craves to see her again. By night he creeps stealthily to the miller's home to watch the happy family through the window.

> .... Philip's dwelling fronted on the street,
> The latest house to landward; but behind,
> With one small gate that open'd on the waste,
> Flourish'd a little garden square and wall'd:
> And in it throve an ancient evergreen,
> A yew tree, and all round it ran a walk
> Of shingle, and a walk divided it:
> But Enoch shunn'd the middle walk and stole
> Up by the wall, behind the yew; and thence
> That which he better might have shunn'd, if griefs
> Like his have worse or better, Enoch saw.

For cups and silver on the burnish'd board
Sparkled and shone; so genial was the hearth:
And on the right hand of the hearth he saw
Philip, the slight suitor of old times,
Stout, rosy, with his babe across his knees;
And o'er her second father stoopt a girl,
A later but a loftier Annie Lee,
Fair-hair'd and tall, and from her lifted hand
Dangled a length of ribbon and a ring
To tempt the babe, who rear'd his creasy arms,
Caught at and ever miss'd it, and they laughed:
And on the left hand of the hearth he saw
The mother glancing often toward her babe,
But turning now and then to speak with him,
Her son, who stood beside her tall and strong,
And saying that which pleased him, for he smiled.

Now when the dead man come to life beheld
His wife his wife no more, and saw the babe
Hers, yet not his, upon the father's knee,
And all the warmth, the peace, the happiness,
And his own children tall and beautiful,
And him, that other, reigning in his place,
Lord of his rights and of his children's love,
Then he, tho' Miriam Lane had told him all,
Because things seen are mightier than things heard,
Stagger'd and shook, holding the branch, and fear'd
To send abroad a shrill and terrible cry,
Which in one moment, like the blast of doom,
Would shatter all the happiness of the hearth.

So he turns away, not wishing to disturb their sublime happiness, and resolving not to make known his identity during his lifetime. Soon he sickens, and recognizing the approach of death, discloses all to Miriam Lane, commanding her to keep his secret until after he is gone.

                            I charge you now,
When you shall see her, tell her that I died
Blessing her, praying for her, loving her;
Save for the bar between us, loving her
As when she laid her head beside my own.
And tell my daughter Annie, whom I saw

> So like her mother, that my latest breath
> Was spent in blessing her and praying for her.
> And tell my son that I died blessing him.
> And say to Philip that I blest him too;
> He never meant us any thing but good.
> But if my children care to see me dead,
> Who hardly knew me living, let them come,
> I am their father; but she must not come,
> For my dead face would vex her after-life.

Enoch Arden dies,
> And when they buried him the little port
> Had seldom seen a costlier funeral.

### Instant Success

*Enoch Arden* was written in only two weeks, and was published in 1864. It was an instant success, some 60,000 copies being sold. In his notes on the poem, Tennyson confessed that its theme was given him by Woolner, the sculptor. "I believe that this particular story came out of Suffolk, but something like the same story is told in Brittany and elsewhere."

Although *Enoch Arden* is imperishable, the little summer-house where it was written, is derelict. However, if you search, as I did, among the grove's tangled vegetation beside Maiden's Croft, you will still find traces of the stone foundations. Stand there a while, and listen, as the Poet did one hundred years before, and you will hear "so loud a calling of the sea."

(Tennyson also composed *The Holy Grail* in the Maiden's Croft summer-house. See page 67.)

# SUNSET AND EVENING STAR

CARLYLE had described Tennyson once as "one of the finest looking men in the world—a great shock of rough dusky dark hair; bright, laughing, hazel eyes; massive aquiline face, most massive yet most delicate; of sallow, brown complexion, almost Indian looking; clothes cynically loose, free-and-easy, smokes infinite tobacco. His voice is musical, metallic, fit for loud laughter and piercing wail, and all that may lie between; speech and speculation free and plenteous; I do not meet in these late decades such company over a pipe! We shall see what he shall grow to."

What, indeed, in his eighty-first year, had he grown to? The Poet asked himself the very same question, as he sat motionless at his desk in the high-backed wooden chair.

It was twilight, and the Farringford study slowly filled with deepening shadows. The two candles on the desk remained unlit. Between his fingers he held a scrap of paper, but he could no longer read the words written on it. No need to—they were branded indelibly on his memory.

Though normally he composed slowly, the lines this time had come to him in a flash of divine inspiration during a twenty minute ferry-crossing of the Solent from Lymington to Yarmouth. Without mentioning them to anyone he had jotted them down on an old envelope, and in his study just now had copied them out afresh with minor corrections.

He had been very near to death in the past few months, and his recovery had seemed miraculous. Indeed, Nurse Durham, who cared for him, had suggested he wrote a hymn of thanksgiving, but instead he composed himself to see his "Pilot face to face." Time for him, he believed, was running out.

At that moment Nurse Durham herself tapped gently on the study door and entered. She saw the Poet silhouetted against the casement windows, and moved to light the candles. After they were lit, Tennyson looked at her, and referring to the suggested hymn of thanksgiving, asked, "Will this do for you, old woman?"

Then he spoke the words in a subdued monotone:

### CROSSING THE BAR

Sunset and evening star,
    And one clear call for me.
And may there be no moaning of the bar,
    When I put out to sea,

But such a tide as moving seems asleep,
    Too full for sound and foam,
When that which drew from out the boundless deep
    Turns again home.

Twilight and evening bell,
    And after that the dark.
And may there be no sadness of farewell,
    When I embark!

For tho' from out our bourne of Time and Place
    The flood may bear me far,
I hope to see my Pilot face to face
    When I have crost the bar.

The words shocked Nurse Durham immeasurably. Patently, the Poet was reciting his own death song. Too choked to speak, she turned away and went out. But Tennyson did not move, and even failed to notice she had left the study, so deeply was he engrossed with his thoughts.

Sunset and evening star,
    And one clear call for me.
And may there be no moaning of the bar,
    When I put out to sea.

Let's face it, he seems to say. I have been ill, very ill, and I am an old man. I cannot have long to live. There's no point in trying to deny that "one clear call." I am prepared for death, and pray only that I may have the strength of courage to go to my Maker without bitterness and regret, and with unswerving faith.

> But such a tide as moving seems asleep,
>     Too full for sound and foam,
> When that which drew from out the boundless deep
>     Turns again home.

Spiritually he is a full man. His gratitude to God for curing him miraculously of his illness is too deeply felt to be expressed adequately in words. The flood tide which originally bore his soul to the shores of Life is now ebbing, returning it to the boundless depths of the Eternal from whence it carne.

> Twilight and evening bell,
>     And after that the dark!
> And may there be no sadness of farewell,
>     When I embark!

Life's decline, and then the end. Here he speaks to his dear ones, beseeching them not to be sad at the last; to have courage enough to overcome the sadness of personal loss, just as he had also done after the deaths of Hallam, Lushington, Simeon, and his own son Lionel.

> For tho' from out our bourne of Time and Place
>     The flood may bear me far,
> I hope to see my Pilot face to face,
>     When I have crost the Bar.

For though in death he will be far away from them, beyond their mortal dimensions of Time and Place, at least they should seek consolation in the fact that he, in spirit, hoped to see his God face to face.

It has already been said that, although the Poet had attained great reverence for the past, his reverence for the present "as containing in it an immediate inspiration and revelation of God," was even greater. This is shown conspicuously in the poem, *Crossing the Bar*, in which his inspiration is fired by a divine faith in the *living* God. His Muse is like the magnificently aspiring lark rising higher and higher above the Mortal plain into the rarefied atmosphere of the Eternal . . . .

**Crown of Life's Work**

At last Tennyson rose and went down from the study to dine with his family. And after dinner, he showed his son, Hallam, the poem. He was quite obviously moved by it, and exclaimed involuntarily, "That is the crown of your life's work!"

"It came in a moment," the Poet replied modestly, and went on to explain that the "Pilot" was "That Divine and Unseen Who is always guiding us."

Hallam tells us in his *Memoir* that a few days before the Poet's death at Aldworth, near Haslemere, he called him to the bedside and said: "Mind you put *Crossing the Bar* at the end of all editions of my poems."

# KING ALFRED

ONE of Tennyson's greatest gifts was that of friendship. His all-embracing wisdom, but essential simplicity, attracted to him men and women of all classes and walks of life. His poetry was read and enjoyed by all, from the ruling Queen to the humblest shepherd. And very soon after his arrival at Farringford, his home became the Mecca for pilgrims from the world over—royalty, statesmen, philosophers, scientists, actors, singers, painters, historians, authors, poets and churchmen. At the oracular fount of course was Alfred Tennyson, or King Alfred as he was playfully called by close friends.

**Shades of Great Men and Women**
Great men had sat in the Farringford study with him, smoking limitless tobacco, exchanging anecdotes and discussing art, religion, philosophy, geology, astronomy and every conceivable subject. And, entranced by the Poet's "God-gifted organ-voice," as he recited passages from his universally known works, they had felt themselves to be in the presence of greatness. Perhaps they had sensed too, that in years to come, later generations would respect them not merely for their own contributions to Art, Science and Religion, but also for that aura of reflected glory as having been intimates of the Poet in his home.

**Unwelcome Visitors**
But universal fame had its disadvantages. By 1867 the Poet's work had become so widely known that sightseers and autograph-hunters, even from as far as the United States, began to invade his privacy. The late Mr. Walters, who had been a family retainer at Farringford since about 1905 and who in 1949 (when I met him) was living in a small cottage opposite the main gates of the estate, told me that one such intrusion aroused the Poet to fury.

He was sitting at work in his study, and happened to glance through the windows at the trees beyond. There he saw a stranger, squatting among the branches of a pine, watching him. He shouted at him to go away, but he would not. Livid with rage, Tennyson summoned a servant and ordered him to chase away the intruder, and afterwards to cut down the tree.

On his walks to High Down, Tennyson was continually harassed by autograph-hunters, who waited at the back garden gate near the wooden bridge; thereafter he always used the bridge itself, and would run across it to escape being noticed. People waiting below would just glimpse the wide-awake hat and the flapping military cloak.

In later years, said Walters, Tennyson became quite abrupt to unwelcome visitors, and was sometimes uncomfortably personal to guests at the dinner table. Quite often, when the Poet did not wish to see anybody, he fled up the turret steps to lock himself in his study. He once refused to see a party of tourists from America, but when rebuked by a friend, who said they had come three thousand miles to see a lion not a bear, he laughingly relented and went to meet them.

The Poet was short-sighted, and on one occasion he took alarm at the sight of a flock of sheep, mistaking them for tourists. Bad eyesight was also responsible for the Poet catching his hair alight with a candle flame one night, as he closely scrutinised pictures on the staircase, when retiring to bed. A friend with him offered to extinguish the smouldering hair, but the Poet said: "Oh never mind, it depends upon chance burnings."

## Summers at Aldworth

Eventually the intrusions on his privacy became so persistent and annoyed him so much, that he decided to look for a possible building site near Haslemere in the spring of 1867. James Knowles, a notable architect and a great friend of the Poet, happened to be waiting on the railway station platform at Haslemere, when who should appear but Tennyson himself. The reunion was a pleasure for both of them.

"I then introduced my wife to him, and he explained how he came to be there-namely, because he was in search of a site where he might build a cottage to take refuge in from the tourists who made his life a burden to him in the Isle of Wight," recalled James Knowles. "He added, 'You are an architect, why should you not make the plans of it for me?' I said, 'With the greatest possible pleasure, upon one condition that I may act professionally without making any professional charge; for I cannot be paid twice over, and you, Mr. Tennyson, have overpaid me already long ago—in the pleasure and delight your works have given me—for any little work I could do for you.' He protested, but in the end accepted my terms."

The foundation-stone of Aldworth was laid on Shakespeare's birthday, April 23rd, 1868, on what used to be a potato-patch. What was to have been a four-roomed cottage, soon became a substantial dwelling with idyllic views of wooded Sussex, the South Downs and the sea. And here, for the remaining years of his life he spent his summers, while Farringford was used for the winter months. And it was while returning to Farringford in October of 1889, that *Crossing the Bar* had come to him.

**Poet's Relics at Farringford**
During the absence of the Tennyson family, and for a period of time after the death of Hallam, Lord Tennyson in 1928, Mr. Walters was left in charge of Farringford. And for eleven years, he said, he attempted the upkeep of the building. Later it was bought and turned into a hotel, and as such I first saw it in 1949.

The house then seemed to be in remarkably good state of repair, and many of the Poet's possessions, though by no means all, were on view to the public. The study in particular, was very much as Tennyson must have left it, and in it I spent the whole of one day examining his relics, a few of which are listed below.

The view from the drawing-room window now is not, perhaps, as magnificent as it had been in the Poet's day, but is nevertheless memorable. A row of tall trees, nearer the sea, now partially obscures Freshwater Bay, although a view of Compton Bay, and the "sea of Mediterranean blue, with rosy capes beyond," as far as Blackgang Chine, can still be enjoyed.

As the study has more recently been redecorated and modernised, and some of the relics have been removed, a mention of the latter may be of value to students of Tennyson's life and work:

**The Study:**
The high-backed wooden chair; his quill and blotter; a large number of books; two Japanese screens; a number of framed photographs of Tennyson, his family, and one or two of them taken in the grounds of Farringford; an ink sketch of "Pyramus and Thisbe, Tennyson's big dog and Puggie, exchanging vows with the glass between"; a collection of photographs depicting Bad Enderby Village and Somers by Rectory and Church; a musical box which played "Sweet Marie," "After the Ball" "All in a Row," "Catholique, Marche," "The Ship I Love," "The Maggie Murphy's Home" and "The Mikado," by Sullivan, Tennyson's friend who often played on the piano at Farringford; Sir John Millais's famous "The Gardener's Daughter"; a pen drawing of Emily Tennyson, by G. F. Watts; "The Lord of Burleigh" set to music, by Frances Ann Gill; an excerpt from Maud illuminated with hand-painted floral designs; a boomerang and a small table hammer, presented to Lady Tennyson by the Adelaide Rowing Club in April, 1900; three poems by Tennyson, decorated with embroidery in beautifully worked colours on fine silk cloth, presented to him after his visit to Coventry; and many other items too numerous to mention here.

**The Hallway:**
A list of famous visitors to Farringford (with a few additions of my own):

>Prince Alamayu of Abyssinia (son of the ill-fated King Theodore)
>William Allingham—Poet
>Mary Anderson—Actress
>George D. Campbell—Statesman and Scientist
>H.R.H. Princess Beatrice
>Edward White Benson—Archbishop of Canterbury
>James (Viscount) Bryce, O.M.—Historian and Statesman

Lewis Carroll—Author of the *Alice* books
Arthur Hugh Clough—Poet
H.R.H. Prince Consort
Charles Darwin—Scientist
Richard Doyle—"Punch" artist
Marquis of Dufferin and Ava—Viceroy of India
Emma-Queen of the Sandwich Islands
Edward FitzGerald—Translator of *Omar Khayyam*
Garibaldi—Italian Patriot
Sir George Groves—Musical Historian
Lord Hatherley—Lord Chancellor
Hubert Herkomer, R.A—Artist
Oliver Wendell Holmes—American Poet
W. Holman Hunt—Artist
Benjamin Jowett—Scholar and Philosopher
Charles Kingsley—Poet and Novelist
Edward Lear—Artist and Nonsense Poet
W. E. H. Lecky—Philosopher and Historian
Longfellow—American Poet
Jenny Lind—Singer
F. D. Maurice—Philosopher and Theologian
J. E. Millais, P.R.A—Artist
Richard Owen—Surgeon and Biologist
F. T. Palgrave—Compiler of the *Golden Treasury*
Sir Hubert Parry—Musical Composer
Coventry Patmore—Poet
Sir Charles Villiers Stanford—Composer
Sir Arthur Sullivan—Composer
Charles Sumner—American Statesman
A. C. Swinburne—Poet
Bayard Taylor—American Poet and Essayist
Ellen Terry—Actress
John Tyndall—Natural Philosopher
G. F. Watts, R.A.—Painter
Samuel Wilberforce—Bishop of Oxford and Winchester
Thomas Woolner, R.A.—Sculptor.

There was also a framed transcription of *Tears, Idle Tears*. Sir Charles Tennyson tells me that he believes these lines were copied out by his elder brother.

## TEARS, IDLE TEARS

Tears, idle tears, I know not what they mean,
Tears from the depth of some divine despair
Rise in the heart, and gather to the eyes,
In looking on the happy Autumn-fields,
And thinking of the days that are no more.

Fresh as the first beam glittering on a sail,
That brings our friends up from the underworld,
Sad as the last which reddens over one
That sinks with all we love below the verge;
So sad, so fresh, the days that are no more.

Ah, sad and strange as in dark summer dawns
The earliest pipe of half-awaken'd birds
To dying ears, when unto dying eyes
The casement slowly grows a glimmering square;
So sad, so strange, the days that are no more.

Dear as remember'd kisses after death,
And sweet as those by hopeless fancy feign'd
On lips that are for others; deep as love,
Deep as first love, and wild with all regret;
O Death in Life, the days that are no more.

# MEMOIRS OF FRIENDS AND NEIGHBOURS OF FARRINGFORD

I.—From **Tennyson and Bradley**, by Margaret L. Woods

GRANVILLE BRADLEY was twelve years younger than Alfred Tennyson; an interval in age which permits at once of veneration and of intimacy. It was at the Lushingtons' house that my father, as an undergraduate of one-and-twenty, first met the young Poet, and became his admirer; but it was not until twelve years later that the admirer became also the friend.

My mother tells in her diary how in that summer of the birthday meeting, the two men roamed the country together, poetizing, botanizing, geologizing. The enthusiasm of science had begun to seize on all thinking humanity, and if botany was considered the only suitable science for ladies, geology had something like a boom among the privileged males. I can see my father now, a slight, active little figure, armed with a hammer and girt with a capacious knapsack, setting forth joyous as a chamois-hunter, for a day's sport among the fossils of the Isle of Wight cliffs. But above all it was the communion of spirit, the play of ideas which interested the two and drew them together. "They talked from 12 noon to 10 p.m., almost incessantly, this day," writes my mother, "Tennyson walking back with him (some three miles) to the Warren Farm, still talking."

One pictures the tall, long-cloaked Bard and the vivacious little scholar pacing side by side, inconscient of time and distance, down the shingly drive of Farringford, through the warm and dusky night of the deep-hedged lanes, overhung with the heavy darkness of August trees, until they came out on the clear pale spaces of the open seaward land, and the whisper and the scent of the sea. And one would guess this to be a picture of two very young men, absorbed in the first joy of one of the romantic friendships of youth, did one not know that the Poet was a man of middle age and the scholar in the maturing thirties . . . .

Those passages in my mother's diary in which she speaks of the happiness it gave my father and herself to make acquaintance with the Poet, and to find him just what they would have wished him to be, have already appeared in the Biography. Also her description of those evenings in the Farringford drawing-room, so often recurring and through so many years, when he would "talk of what was in his heart," or read aloud some poem, often yet unpublished, while they listened, looking out on the lovely landscape and the glimpse of the sea which, "framed in the dark-arched bow-window," seemed, like some beautiful picture, almost to form part of the room . . . .

I see now the long Farringford drawing-room, full of the green shade of a cedar tree which grew near the great window, and the slight figure of Lady Tennyson rising from the red sofa—it was a red room—and gliding towards my mother with a smile upon her lips. She always wore a soft gray cashmere gown, and it was always made in the same simple fashion; much as dresses were worn in the days of Cruikshank . . . . Her silky auburn-brown hair, partly hidden by lace lappets, was untouched with gray, and her complexion kept its rose-leaf delicacy, just as her strong and cultivated intellect kept its alertness, to the last days of her life. No sooner were the greetings over than ten to one the door would open, and the Poet would come slowly, softly, silently, into the room, dressed in an old-fashioned black tail-coat, and fixing my mother with his distant short-sighted gaze. One day, she being seated with her back to the cedar-green window, he approached her with such extreme deference, and so solemn a courtesy, as made her all amazed; until in a minute, with a flash of amusement, both discovered that he had mistaken her for—the Queen. Still more surely one or both of the long-haired, gray-tunicked boys would appear, less silently; and away the children scampered to their endless play about the rambling house and grounds. But even the children's play was informed with the vital interest of the two houses: the story of King Arthur and his knights. The first *Idylls of the King* had appeared, and others were appearing. It was a red-letter evening indeed when Poet and new poem were ready for a reading, either in the little upstairs study, or in the drawing-room, where dessert was always laid after dinner, and he sat at the head of the round table in a high carved chair . . . .

I remember now a story of Tennyson's which tickled my childish sense of humour exceedingly, the point of it lying in a bit of bad French, the badness of which I could appreciate. My father had a vein of dry humour, which being akin to that of the Poet, doubtless assisted to knit the bonds of friendship, since to find the same thing humorous is almost essential to real intimacy. There was between the two the natural give-and-take of friendship, and to the warm appreciation given as well as received, Emily Tennyson's letters bear constant witness. "Mr. Bradley's intellectual activity, so warmed by the heart, is very good for my Ally," she writes; and again: "I know you would be pleased if you could hear Ally recur to his talks with Mr. Bradley, and one particular talk about the Resurrection and [illegible]. It is difficult to express admiration, so I won't say any more, except God bless you both."

. . . . .

## II.—From **Recollections of Tennyson**, by the Rev. H. Montagu Butler

. . My real acquaintance with the Tennyson family dates from the end of 1861 and the early days of 1862. My first marriage had been on December 19th, 1861, and a few days afterwards we came to Freshwater, and stayed at the hotel close to the sea, where Dr. and Mrs. Vaughan had sometimes stayed during his Harrow Mastership. It was then that we first met the Granville Bradleys, destined to be our dear friends for life, and it was in their company that we soon found ourselves most kindly welcomed guests at Farringford.

The two first incidents that I remember were the Poet showing us the proof of his *Dedication of the Idylls*, and, at our request, reading out to us *Enoch Arden*. The *Dedication* must have been composed almost immediately after the death of the Prince Consort on December 14th. He seemed himself pleased with it. I thought at the time, and I have felt ever since, that these lines rank high, not only among his other tributes of the same kind, but in the literature of epitaphs generally. We felt it a proud privilege to be allowed to stand at his side as he looked over the proof just arrived by the post, and it led us of course to talk sympathetically of the late Prince and the poor widowed Queen.

Very soon after, the Bradleys and we dined at Farringford. The dinner hour was, I think, as early as six, and then, after he had retreated to his *sanctum* for a smoke, he would come down to the drawing-room, and read aloud to his guests. On this occasion he read to us *Enoch Arden*, then only in manuscript. I had before heard much of his peculiar manner of reading, with its deep and often monotonous tones, varied with a sudden lift of the voice as if into the air, at the end of a sentence or a clause. It was, as always, a reading open to criticism on the score of lack of variety, but my dear bride and I were in no mood to criticize. The spell was upon us. Every note of his magnificent voice spoke of majesty or tenderness or awe. It was, in plain words, a prodigious treat to have heard him. We walked back through the winter darkness to our hotel, conscious of having enjoyed a unique privilege.

· · · · ·

### III.—From Tennyson and W. G. Ward and other Farringford Friends, by Wilfred Ward

SPEAKING generally, it was a society in which good breeding, literary taste, general information, and personal distinction counted for much more than worldly or official *status*. I think that we young people looked upon a government official of average endowment as rather an outsider. Genius was all in all for us—officialdom and conventionality in general were unpopular in Freshwater.

Indeed, how could conventionality obtain a footing in a society in which Mrs. Cameron [a pioneer photographer, and an eccentric genius in her own right] and Tennyson were the central figures? I recall Mrs. Cameron pressing my father's hand to her heart, and addressing him as "Squire Ward." I recall her, during her celebrated private theatricals at Dimbola [now Dimbola Lodge Museum, run by the Julia Margaret Cameron Trust], when a distinguished audience tittered at some stage misadventure which occurred during a tragic scene, mounting a chair and insisting loudly and with angry gesticulation, "You must not laugh; you must cry." I recall her bringing Tennyson to my father's house while she was photographing representatives for the characters in the *Idylls of the King*, and calling out directly she saw Cardinal Vaughan (to whom she was a perfect stranger), "Alfred, I have found Sir Lancelot." Tennyson's reply was, "I want a face well worn with evil passion."

My own intercourse with the Poet was chiefly after my father's death in 1882. Tennyson was then an old man who had passed his three score years and ten. His deeply serious mind brooded constantly on the prospect for the future, and the meaning of human life, which was, for him, nearly over.

. . . . .

### IV.—From **Tennyson and Sir John Simeon,** by Louisa E. Ward

THE autumn and winter '71-'72 my eldest brother and I spent together at Freshwater. We rented Mrs. Cameron's little house which opens by a door of communication into the large hall of Dimbola, the house in which she lived. The evening we arrived, she suddenly appeared in our drawing-room saying, "When, strangers take this house I keep the door between us locked, with friends never"; and locked it never was. We lived almost as part of the family, and it was a real enjoyment to be in such close intimacy with one of the most original, and at the same time most tender-hearted and generous women I have ever known. She was on very intimate terms at Farringford, and would speak her mind to the Poet in a very amusing way . . . .

Mrs. Cameron's beautiful white-haired old husband in his royal purple dressing-gown was a most interesting personality. In addition to the large experience of men and things which his many years of official life in India had given him, and which made his society delightful, he was a very fine classical scholar of the old school, and in his old age, when blindness and infirmity debarred him in great measure from his books, it was his solace to repeat by heart odes of Horace, pages of Virgil, and long passages from the Greek poets.

Easter 1872 brought a bright and merry gathering to Freshwater. One of Mrs. Cameron's charming relations (they had lived with her for years as adopted daughters) was about to marry, and go out with her husband to India, and the "Primrose wedding" brought a large influx of young people, friends and relations of Mrs. Cameron and the bride, in addition to the visitors who always made Easter a pleasant time. The weather was perfect, the "April airs that fan the Isle of Wight" especially soft and balmy. Parties of twenty or thirty met every evening in Mrs. Cameron's hall or in the Farringford drawing-room. Nearly everyone there knew or got to know Lord and Lady Tennyson. He was in particularly genial health and spirits; he joined the young people in their midnight walks to the sea, in their flowerseeking expeditions, in one of which someone was fortunate enough to find a grape hyacinth in one of the Farringford fields. He read aloud nearly as much as he was asked to, and danced as vigorously as the youngest present at two dances that were given. It was during the first of these dances that a young neighbour became engaged to the lady whom he shortly afterwards married. Very soon after the decisive moment had passed, and when the event was naturally supposed to be a profound secret, Tennyson put the girl's mother, with whom he happened to be sitting, completely out of countenance by saying, without a suspicion of malice, and without for the moment recognizing the young couple who passed him, "I wot they be two lovyers dear." When he was shortly afterwards told of the engagement, he twinkled very much over his rather premature but very apposite announcement.

My marriage took place in the autumn of 1872, and my husband, who already knew the Tennysons, was at once received into their intimacy, and their friendship was henceforth one of the greatest privileges of our joint life. Tennyson and Hallam were present at our wedding, and the former held our eldest boy in his arms when he was but a day or two old.

The Easter of 1873 saw us again at Freshwater with another pleasant meeting of friends. On that occasion Tennyson said to me, "Why do you not ask me to dinner?" It need not be said that we at once gave the invitation, though not a little nervous at the thought of the lodging-house fare and arrangements to which we were bidding him; but our dear old landlady did her very best. We asked a small party (Lady Florence Herbert and Leslie Stephen* were our guests) to meet him and Hallam; he was himself in the best of spirits, and our little dinner-party proved a great success.

*Later Sir Leslie Stephen, who was the first Editor of the Dictionary of National Biography.

He first married Thackeray's younger daughter, Minnie. Following her untimely death he married Julia Duckworth née Prinsep, niece of Julia Margaret Cameron. As a young girl she had been the model for Marocetti's beautiful figure of King Charles the First's young daughter, Princess Elizabeth in St. Thomas's Church in Newport. Their elder daughter, Vanessa married Clive Bell and their younger daughter, Julia married Leonard Woolf.

# Beyond the Grave
(From **Tennyson: a Memoir,** by Hallam, Lord Tennyson, 1899)

My father was now in his seventy-seventh year. Wendell Holmes, Craik and his other guests were much struck "by his patience under his sorrow [for Lionel, his youngest son, had died in April 1886, during a voyage home from India], and by his unselfish thoughtfulness for others."

Sometimes when he was with us alone he would say, "The thought of Lionel's death tears me to pieces, he was so full of promise and so young"; and "to keep himself up" he worked harder than ever at his new *Locksley Hall*. He was touched by one of the daily papers saying of his Ode *Welcome, welcome with one voice!* sung at the opening of the Colonial Exhibition, that "The twelve thousand people were deeply moved, remembering his sorrow."

The shepherd on our farm [at Farringford] died this spring, an old fellow of ninety-two, with whom he had had many talks. On his tombstone was put, by my father's desire, "God's finger touch'd him and he slept." A little before his death he said: "I should like to see master again; he is a wonderful man for Nature and Life."

In the evenings my father would pace up and down Maiden's Croft, the meadow where *Enoch Arden* and *The Holy Grail* had come into being; he would admire the afterglow on the trees in St. George's (the mediaeval-looking field beyond), and would talk about the stars. The planet Venus was unusually bright, and he would say, "Can you imagine roaring London and raving Paris there in that point of peaceful light?" He would add, "While I said '*there*', the earth has whirled 20 miles."

For his "daily airings" he often drove instead of walking, and favourite drives of his were to Calbourne to see "the huddling brook," or by the old-world thatched cottages of Thorley and Wellow to Newtown creek, or through the fishing-hamlets along the southern coast of the island. "The greatest inventor, it seems to me, must have been the inventor of a wheel," he said to me in one of these drives, during which he would discuss many subjects with great animation. Once he stopped under a telegraph post "to listen to the wail of the wires, the souls of dead messages" . . . .

At the end of the year, as my father was walking with Ralston (the Russian scholar), in Freshwater, he came across an old Wesleyan preacher dead in the road, who had died on his way to the Wesleyan Chapel. My father wrote to one of the near relatives: "I cannot but look upon his death as a happy one; sudden, painless, while he was on his way to his chapel, to render thanks and praise to his Maker. Our Liturgy prays against sudden death; but I myself could pray for such a sudden death as Isaac Porter's."

In December *The Promise of May* and *Locksley Hall Sixty Years After* were published (dated 1887).

*Locksley Hall* was dedicated to my mother, partly because it seemed to my father that the two *Locksley Halls* were likely to be in the future two of the most historically interesting of his poems, as descriptive of the tone of the age at two distinct periods of his life: partly perhaps because the following four lines were written immediately after the death of my brother, and described his chief characteristics:

> Truth, for Truth is Truth, he worshipt, being true as
>     he was brave;
> Good, for Good is Good, he follow'd, yet he look'd beyond
>     the grave!
> Truth for Truth, and Good for Good! The Good, the True,
>     the Pure, the Just!
> Take the charm "For ever" from them and they crumble
>     into dust.

(The Poet speaks of Lionel's death in the poem, *To the Marquis of Dufferin and Ava*; see page 78.)

# SELECTED POEMS PUBLISHED AFTER 1853

## COME INTO THE GARDEN, MAUD

HALLAM TENNYSON described his father's reading of the following passage, thus: "Joy culminates in *Come into the Garden, Maud*, and my father's eyes, which were through the other love-passages veiled by his drooping lids, would suddenly flash as he looked up and spoke these words, the passion in his voice deepening in the words of the stanza"—

> She is coming, my own, my sweet;
>> Were it ever so airy a tread,
>>> etc., etc.

(Part 1. Section XXII, from *Maud*)

### I

Come into the garden, Maud,
  For the black bat, night, has flown,
Come into the garden, Maud,
  I am here at the gate alone;
And the woodbine spices are wafted abroad,
  And the musk of the rose is blown.

### II

For a breeze of morning moves,
  And the planet of Love is on high,
Beginning to faint in the light that she loves
  On a bed of daffodil sky,
To faint in the light of the sun she loves,
  To faint in his light, and to die.

## III

All night have the roses heard
    The flute, violin, bassoon;
All night has the casement jessamine stirr'd
    To the dancers dancing in tune;
Till a silence fell with the waking bird,
    And a hush with the setting moon.

## IV

I said to the lily, "There is but one
    With whom she has heart to be gay.
When will the dancers leave her alone?
    She is weary of dance and play."
Now half to the setting moon are gone,
    And half to the rising day;
Low on the sand and loud on the stone
    The last wheel echoes away.

## V

I said to the rose, "The brief night goes
    In babble and revel and wine.
O young lord-lover, what sighs are those,
    For one that will never be thine?
But mine, but mine," so I sware to the rose,
    "For ever and ever, mine."

## VI

And the soul of the rose went into my blood,
    As the music clash'd in the hall;
And long by the garden lake I stood,
    For I heard your rivulet fall
From the lake to the meadow and on to the wood,
    Our wood, that is dearer than all;

## VII

From the meadow your walks have left so sweet
    That whenever a March-wind sighs
He sets the jewel-print on your feet
    In violets blue as your eyes,
To the woody hollows in which we meet
    And the valleys of Paradise.

## VIII

The slender acacia would not shake
    One long milk-bloom on the tree;
The white lake-blossom fell into the lake
    As the pimpernel dozed on the lea;
But the rose was awake all night for your sake,
    Knowing your promise to me;
The lilies and roses were all awake,
    They sigh'd for the dawn and thee.

## IX

Queen rose of the rosebud garden of girls,
    Come hither, the dances are done,
In gloss of satin and glimmer of pearls,
    Queen lily and rose in one;
Shine out, little head, sunning over with curls,
    To the flowers, and be their sun.

## X

There has fallen a splendid tear
    From the passion-flower at the gate.
She is coming, my dove, my dear;
    She is coming, my life, my fate;
The red rose cries, "She is near, she is near;".
    And the white rose weeps, "She is late;"
The larkspur listens, "I hear, I hear;"
    And the lily whispers, "I wait."

## XI

She is coming, my own, my sweet;
    Were it ever so airy a tread,
My heart would hear her and beat,
    Were it earth in an earthy bed;
My dust would hear her and beat,
    Had I lain for a century dead;
Would start and tremble under her feet,
    And blossom in purple and red.

# THE HOLY GRAIL (Extract)

LIKE *Enoch Arden, The Holy Grail* was composed in the little summerhouse Tennyson built himself on Maiden's Croft, at the back of Farringford. In the following passage, Sir Lancelot, when asked by King Arthur what the quest for the Holy Grail has availed him, answers:

" 'O King, my friend, if friend of thine I be,
Happier are those that welter in their sin,
Swine in the mud, that cannot see for slime,
Slime of the ditch: but in me lived a sin
So strange, of such a kind, that all of pure,
Noble, and knightly in me twined and clung
Round that one sin, until the wholesome flower
And poisonous grew together, each as each,
Not to be pluck'd asunder; and when thy knights
Sware, I sware with them only in the hope
That could I touch or see the Holy Grail
They might be pluck'd asunder. Then I spake
To one most holy saint, who wept and said,
That save they could be pluck'd asunder, all
My quest were but in vain; to whom I vow'd
That I would work according as he will'd.
And forth I went, and while I yearn'd and strove
To tear the twain asunder in my heart,
My madness came upon me as of old,
And whipt me into waste fields far away;
There was I beaten down by little men,
Mean knights, to whom the moving of my sword
And shadow of my spear had been enow
To scare them from me once; and then I came
All in my folly to the naked shore,
Wide flats, where nothing but coarse grasses grew;
But such a blast, my King, began to blow,
So loud a. blast along the shore and sea,
Ye could not hear the waters for the blast,
Tho' heapt in mounds and ridges all the sea

Drove like a cataract, and all the sand
Swept like a river, and the clouded heavens
Were shaken with the motion and the sound.
And blackening in the sea-foam sway'd a boat
Half-swallow'd in it, anchor'd with a chain;
And in my madness to myself I said,
"I will embark and I will lose myself,
And in the great sea wash away my sin."
I burst the chain, I sprang into the boat.
Seven days I drove along the dreary deep,
And with me drove the moon and all the stars;
And the wind fell, and on the seventh night
I heard the shingle grinding in the surge,
And felt the boat shock earth, and looking up,
Behold, the enchanted towers of Carbonek,
A castle like a rock upon a rock,
With chasm-like portals open to the sea,
And steps that met the breaker! there was none
Stood near it but a lion on each side
That kept the entry, and the moon was full.
Then from the boat I leapt, and up the stairs.
There drew my sword. With sudden-flaring manes
Those two great beasts rose upright like a man,
Each gript a shoulder, and I stood between;
And, when I would have smitten them, heard a voice,
"Doubt not, go forward; if thou doubt, the beasts
Will tear thee piecemeal." Then with violence
The sword was dash'd from out my hand, and fell.
And up into the sounding hall I past;
But nothing in the sounding hall I saw,
No bench nor table, painting on the wall
Or shield of knight; only the rounded moon
Thro' the tall oriel on the rolling sea.
But always in the quiet house I heard,
Clear as a lark, high o'er me as a lark,
A sweet voice singing in the topmost tower
To the eastward; up I climb'd a thousand steps
With pain: as in a dream I seem'd to climb
For ever: at the last I reach'd a door,
A light was in the crannies, and I heard,
"Glory and joy and honour to our Lord
And to the Holy Vessel of the Grail."
Then in my madness I essay'd the door;

It gave; and thro' a stormy glare, a heat
As from a seven times-heated furnace, I,
Blasted and burnt, and blinded as I was,
With such a fierceness that I swoon'd away—
O, yet methought I saw the Holy Grail,
All pall'd in crimson samite, and around
Great angels, awful shapes, and wings and eyes.
And but for all my madness and my sin,
And then my swooning, I had sworn I saw
That which I saw; but what I saw was veil'd
And cover'd; and this Quest was not for me.'

"So speaking, and here ceasing, Lancelot left
The hall long silent, till Sir Gawain—nay,
Brother, I need not tell thee foolish words,—
A reckless and irreverent knight was he,
Now bolden'd by the silence of his King,—
Well, I will tell thee: 'O King, my liege,' he said,
'Hath Gawain fail'd in any quest of thine?
When have I stinted stroke in foughten field?
But as for thine, my good friend Percivale,
Thy holy nun and thou have driven men mad,
Yea, made our mightiest madder than our least.
But by mine eyes and by mine ears I swear,
I will be deafer than the blue-eyed cat,
And thrice as blind as any noonday owl,
To holy virgins in their ecstasies,
Henceforward.'

" 'Deafer,' said the blameless King,
'Gawain, and blinder unto holy things
Hope not to make thyself by idle vows,
Being too blind to have desire to see.
But if indeed there came a sign from heaven,
Blessed are Bors, Lancelot and Percivale,
For these have seen according to their sight
For every fiery prophet in old times,
And all the sacred madness of the bard,
When God made music thro' them, could but speak
His music by the framework and the chord;
And as ye saw it ye have spoken truth.

" 'Nay—but thou errest, Lancelot: never yet
Could all of true and noble in knight and man

Twine round one sin, whatever it might be,
With such a closeness, but apart there grew,
Save that he were the swine thou spakest of,
Some root of knighthood and pure nobleness;
Whereto see thou, that it may bear its flower.

  " 'And spake I not too truly, O my knights?
Was I too dark a prophet when I said
To those who went upon the Holy Quest,
That most of them would follow wandering fires,
Lost in the quagmire?—lost to me and gone,
And left me gazing at a barren board,
And a lean Order-scarce return'd a tithe—
And out of those to whom the vision came
My greatest hardly will believe he saw;
Another hath beheld it afar off,
And leaving human wrongs to right themselves,
Cares but to pass into the silent life.
And one hath had the vision face to face,
And now his chair desires him here in vain,
However they may crown him otherwhere.

  " 'And some among you held, that if the King
Had seen the sight he would have sworn the vow:
Not easily, seeing that the King must guard
That which he rules, and is but as the hind
To whom a space of land is given to plough,
Who may not wander from the allotted field
Before his work be done; but, being done,
Let visions of the night or of the day
Come, as they will; and many a time they come,
Until this earth he walks on seems not earth,
This light that strikes his eyeball is not light,
This air that smites his forehead is not air
But vision—yea, his very hand and foot—
In moments when he feels he cannot die,
And knows himself no vision to himself,
Nor the high God a vision, nor that One
Who rose again: ye have seen what ye have seen.'

  "So spake the King: I knew not all he meant."

# THE PASSING OF ARTHUR (Extract)

THE following passage from *The Passing of Arthur* is almost an exact replica of the earlier *Morte d' Arthur*, published in "Poems, 1842," with only minor alterations in punctuation and stanza spacing:

So all day long the noise of battle roll'd
Among the mountains by the winter sea;
Until King Arthur's Table, man by man,
Had fall'n in Lyonnesse about their lord,
King Arthur. Then, because his wound was deep,
The bold Sir Bedivere uplifted him,
And bore him to a chapel nigh the field,
A broken chancel with a broken cross,
That stood on a dark strait of barren land:
On one side lay the Ocean, and on one
Lay a great water, and the moon was full.

Then spake King Arthur to Sir Bedivere:
"The sequel of today unsolders all
The goodliest fellowship of famous knights
Whereof this world holds record. Such a sleep
They sleep—the men I loved. I think that we
Shall never more, at any future time,
Delight our souls with talk of knightly deeds,
Walking about the gardens and the halls
Of Camelot, as in the days that were.
I perish by this people which I made,—
Tho' Merlin sware that I should come again
To rule once more; but, let what will be, be,
I am so deeply smitten thro' the helm
That without help I cannot last till morn.
Thou therefore take my brand Excalibur,
Which was my pride: for thou rememberest how
In those old days, one summer noon, an arm
Rose up from out the bosom of the lake,
Clothed in white samite, mystic, wonderful,

Holding the sword—and how I row'd across
And took it, and have worn it, like a king:
And, wheresoever I am sung or told
In aftertime, this also shall be known:
But now delay not: take Excalibur,
And fling him far into the middle mere:
Watch what thou seest, and lightly bring me word."

   To him replied the bold Sir Bedivere:
"It is not meet, Sir King, to leave thee thus,
Aidless, alone, and smitten thro' the helm—
A little thing may harm a wounded man;
Yet I thy hest will all perform at full,
Watch what I see, and lightly bring thee word."

   So saying, from the ruin'd shrine he stept,
And in the moon athwart the place of tombs,
Where lay the mighty bones of ancient men,
Old knights, and over them the sea-wind sang
Shrill, chill, with flakes of foam. He, stepping down
By zig-zag paths, and juts of pointed rock,
Came on the shining levels of the lake.

   There drew he forth the brand Excalibur,
And o'er him, drawing it, the winter moon,
Brightening the skirts of a long cloud, ran forth
And sparkled keen with frost against the hilt:
For all the haft twinkled with diamond sparks,
Myriads of topaz-lights, and jacinth-work
Of subtless jewellery. He gazed so long
That both his eyes were dazzled, as he stood,
This way and that dividing the swift mind,
In act to throw: but at the last it seem'd
Better to leave Excalibur conceal'd
There in the many-knotted waterflags,
That whistled stiff and dry about the marge.
So strode he back slow to the wounded King.

   Then spake King Arthur to Sir Bedivere:
"Hast thou perform'd my mission which I gave?
What is it thou hast seen? or what hast heard?"

   And answer made the bold Sir Bedivere:
"I heard the ripple washing in the reeds,
And the wild water lapping on the crag."

To whom replied King Arthur, faint and pale:
"Thou hast betray'd thy nature and thy name,
Not rendering true answer, as beseem'd
Thy fealty, nor like a noble knight:
For surer sign had follow'd, either hand,
Or voice, or else a motion of the mere.
This is a shameful thing for men to lie.
Yet now, I charge thee, quickly go again,
As thou art lief and dear, and do the thing
I bade thee, watch, and lightly bring me word."

Then went Sir Bedivere the second time
Across the ridge, and paced beside the mere,
Counting the dewy pebbles, fix'd in thought;
But when he saw the wonder of the hilt,
How curiously and strangely chased, he smote
His palms together, and he cried aloud:

"And if indeed I cast the brand away,
Surely a precious thing, one worthy note,
Should thus be lost for ever from the earth,
Which might have pleased the eyes of many men.
What good should follow this, if this were done?
What harm, undone? Deep harm to disobey,
Seeing obedience is the bond of rule.
Were it well to obey then, if a king demand
An act unprofitable, against himself?.
The King is sick, and knows not what he does.
What record, or what relic of my lord,
Should be to aftertime, but empty breath
And rumours of a doubt? But were this kept,
Stored in some treasure-house of mighty kings,
Some one might show it at a joust of arms,
Saying, 'King Arthur's sword, Excalibur,
Wrought by the lonely maiden of the Lake.
Nine years she wrought it, sitting in the deeps
Upon the hidden bases of the hills.'
So might some old man speak in the aftertime
To all the people, winning reverence.
But now much honour and much fame were lost."

So spake he, clouded with his own conceit,
And hid Excalibur the second time,
And so strode back slow to the wounded King.

Then spoke King Arthur, breathing heavily:
"What is it thou hast seen? or what hast heard?"

And answer made the bold Sir Bedivere:
"I heard the water lapping on the crag,
And the long ripple washing in the reeds."

To whom replied King Arthur, much in wrath:
"Ah, miserable and unkind, untrue,
Unknightly, traitor-hearted! Woe is me!
Authority forgets a dying king,
Laid widow'd of the power in his eye
That bow'd the will. I see thee what thou art,
For thou, the latest-left of all my knights,
In whom should meet the offices of all,
Thou wouldst betray me for the precious hilt;
Either from lust of gold, or like a girl
Valuing the giddy pleasure of the eyes.
Yet, for a man may fail in duty twice,
And the third time may prosper, get thee hence:
But, if thou spare to fling Excalibur,
I will arise and slay thee with my hands."

Then quickly rose Sir Bedivere, and ran,
And, leaping down the ridges lightly, plunged
Among the bulrush-beds, and clutch'd the sword,
And strongly wheel'd and threw it. The great brand
Made lightnings in the splendour of the moon,
And flashing round and round, and whirl'd in an arch,
Shot like a streamer of the northern morn,
Seen where the moving isles of winter shock
By night, with noises of the northern sea.
So flash'd and fell the brand Excalibur:
But ere he dipt the surface, rose an arm
Clothed in white samite, mystic, wonderful,
And caught him by the hilt, and brandish'd him
Three times, and drew him under in-the mere.
And lightly went the other to the King.

Then spoke King Arthur, drawing thicker breath:
"Now see I by thine eyes that this is done.
Speak out: what is it thou hast heard, or seen?"

And answer made the bold Sir Bedivere:
"Sir King, I closed mine eyelids, lest the gems
Should blind my purpose, for I never saw,
Nor shall see, here or elsewhere, till I die,
Not tho' I live three lives of mortal men,
So great a miracle as yonder hilt.
Then with both hands I flung him, wheeling him;
But when I look'd again, behold an arm,
Clothed in white samite, mystic, wonderful,
That caught him by the hilt, and brandish'd him
Three times, and drew him under in the mere."

And answer made King Arthur, breathing hard:
"My end draws nigh; 'tis time that I were gone.
Make broad thy shoulders to receive my weight,
And bear me to the margin; yet I fear
My wound hath taken cold, and I shall die."

So saying, from the pavement he half rose,
Slowly, with pain, reclining on his arm,
And looking wistfully with wide blue eyes
As in a picture. Him Sir Bedivere
Remorsefully regarded thro' his tears,
And would have spoken, but he found not words;
Then took with care, and kneeling on one knee,
O'er both his shoulders drew the languid hands,
And rising bore him thro' the place of tombs.

But, as he walk'd, King Arthur panted hard,
Like one that feels a nightmare on his bed
When all the house is mute. So sigh'd the King,
Muttering and murmuring at his ear "Quick, quick!
I fear it is too late, and I shall die."
But the other swiftly strode from ridge to ridge,
Clothed with his breath, and looking, as he walk'd,
Larger than human on the frozen hills.
He heard the deep behind him, and a cry
Before. His own thought drove him like a goad.
Dry clash'd his harness in the icy caves
And barren chasms, and all to left and right
The bare black cliff clang'd round him, as he based
His feet on juts of slippery crag that rang
Sharp-smitten with the dint of armed heels—

And on a sudden, lo! the level lake,
And the long glories of the winter moon.

    Then saw they how there hove a dusky barge,
Dark as a funeral scarf from stern to stern,
Beneath them; and descending they were ware
That all the decks were dense with stately forms,
Black-stoled, black-hooded, like a dream—by these
Three Queens with crowns of gold: and from them rose
A cry that shiver'd to the tingling stars,
And, as it were one voice, an agony
Of lamentation, like a wind that shrills
All night in a waste land, where no one comes,
Or hath come, since the making of the world.

    Then murmur'd Arthur, "Place me in the barge;"
So to the barge they came. There those three Queens
Put forth their hands, and took the King, and wept.
But she, that rose the tallest of them all
And fairest, laid his head upon her lap,
And loosed the shatter'd casque, and chafed his hands,
And call'd him by his name, complaining loud,
And dropping bitter tears against his brow
Striped with dark blood: for all his face was white
And colourless, and like the wither'd moon
Smote by the fresh beam of the springing east;
And all his greaves and cuisses dash'd with drops
Of onset; and the light and lustrous curls—
That made his forehead like a rising sun
High from the dais-throne—were parch'd with dust;
Or, clotted into points and hanging loose,
Mix'd with the knightly growth that fringed his lips.
So like a shatter'd column lay the King;
Not like that Arthur who, with lance in rest,
From spur to plume a star of tournament,
Shot thro' the lists at Camelot, and charged
Before the eyes of ladies and of kings.

    Then loudly cried the bold Sir Bedivere:
"Ah! my Lord Arthur, whither shall I go?
Where shall I hide my forehead and my eyes?
For now I see the true old times are dead,
When every morning brought a noble chance,

And every chance brought out a noble knight.
Such times have been not since the light that led
The holy Elders with the gift of myrrh.
But now the whole Round Table is dissolved
Which was an image of the mighty world;
And I, the last, go forth companionless,
And the days darken round me, and the years,
Among new men, strange faces, other minds."

   And slowly answered Arthur from the barge:
"The old order changeth, yielding place to new,
And God fulfils himself in many ways,
Lest one good custom should corrupt the world.
Comfort thyself: what comfort is in me?
I have lived my life, and that which I have done
May He within Himself make pure! but thou,
If thou shouldst never see my face again,
Pray for my soul. More things are wrought by prayer
Than this world dreams of. Wherefore, let thy voice
Rise like a fountain for me night and day.
For what are men better than sheep or goats
That nourish a blind life within the brain,
If, knowing God, they lift not hands of prayer
Both for themselves and those who call them friend?
For so the whole round earth is every way
Bound by gold chains about the feet of God.
But now farewell. I am going a long way
With these thou seest—if indeed I go
(For all my mind is clouded with a doubt)—
To the island-valley of Avilion;
Where falls not hail, or rain, or any snow,
Nor ever wind blows loudly; but it lies
Deep-meadow'd, happy, fair with orchard-lawns
And bowery hollows crown'd with summer sea,
Where I will heal me of my grievous wound."

   So said he, and the barge with oar and sail
Moved from the brink, like some full-breasted swan
That, fluting a wild carol ere her death,
Ruffles her pure cold plume, and takes the flood
With swarthy webs. Long stood Sir Bedivere
Revolving many memories, till the hull
Look'd one black dot against the verge of dawn,
And on the mere the wailing died away.

In the poem, *To the Marquis of Dufferin and Ava*, Tennyson speaks of the death at sea of Lionel, his youngest son, when returning home from India.

Lionel served in the India Office, and "his Blue Book on India," wrote his brother, "is a model of clear style and condensation. As a relaxation from official work he wrote articles for magazines, and for the *Saturday Review*, and occasional poems, and took a great interest in music for the working classes. In 1885 at the invitation of Lord Dufferin he went with his wife (Eleanor) on a tour of India, in order to see as much of the country as he could for himself. The part of his tour which he seemed to enjoy most was that in the old-world Rajputana. While shooting in Assam he caught jungle-fever. The poison was in his system when he attended the camp of exercise at Delhi, where during the military manoeuvres he was exposed to very inclement weather. On his return to Calcutta he fell dangerously ill, and never recovered, but hung between life and death for three months and a half, bearing his suffering with the utmost fortitude and with uncomplaining resignation . . . . He started for home from Calcutta at the beginning of April. Then came the last days on the Red Sea. He spoke little and did not suffer much pain. He passed away peacefully at three in the afternoon on April 20th. The burial service was at nine that same evening, under a great silver moon. The ship stopped: and the coffin was lowered into the phosphorescent sea."

## TO THE MARQUIS OF DUFFERIN AND AVA

At times our Britain cannot rest,
   At times her steps are swift and rash;
   She moving, at her girdle clash
The golden keys of East and West.

Not swift or rash, when late she lent
   The sceptres of her West, her East,
   To one, that ruling has increased
Her greatness and her self-content.

Your rule has made the people love
   Their ruler. Your viceregal days
   Have added fulness to the phrase
Of "Gauntlet in the velvet glove."

But since your name will grow with Time,
   Not all, as honouring your fair fame
   Of Statesman, have I made the name
A golden portal to my rhyme:

But more, that you and yours may know
   From me and mine, how dear a debt
   We owed you, and are owing yet
To you and yours, and still would owe.

For he (1)—your India was his Fate,
   And drew him over sea to you—
   He fain had ranged her thro' and thro'
To serve her myriads and the State,—

A soul that, watch'd from earliest youth,
   And on thro' many a brightening year,
   Had never swerved for craft or fear,
By one side-path, from simple truth;

Who might have chased and claspt Renown
   And caught her chaplet here—and there
   In haunts of jungle-poison'd air
The flame of life went wavering down;

But ere he left your fatal shore,
   And lay on that funereal boat,
   Dying, "Unspeakable" he wrote
"Their kindness," and he wrote no more;

And sacred is the latest word;
   And now the Was, the Might-have-been,
   And those lone rites I have not seen,
And one drear sound I have not heard,

Are dreams that scarce will let me be,
   Not there to bid my boy farewell,
   When That within the coffin fell,
Fell—and flash'd into the Red Sea,

Beneath a hard Arabian moon
    And alien stars.  To question, why
    The sons before the fathers die,
Not mine! and I may meet him soon;

But while my life's late eve endures,
    Nor settles into hueless gray,
    My memories of his briefer day
Will mix with love for you and yours.

(1) Lionel Tennyson